A Survey of Recent
Christian Ethics

A Survey of Recent Christian Ethics

EDWARD LeROY LONG, Jr.

New York/Oxford
OXFORD UNIVERSITY PRESS
1982

Copyright © 1982 by Oxford University Press, Inc.

LIBRARY OF CONGRESS CATALOGING IN PUBLICATION DATA

Long, Edward LeRoy.
  A survey of recent Christian ethics.

  Bibliography: p.
  Includes index.
  1. Christian ethics—History—20th century.
  I. Title.
  BJ1231.L66   241'.09'048   82-2099
  ISBN 0-19-503159-8   AACR2
  ISBN 0-19-503160-1 (pbk.)

Printing (last digit): 9 8 7 6 5 4 3 2 1

Printed in the United States of America

To Grace
New Companion in
Love, Learning, Labor

Preface

This is a report on the changing contours of Christian thinking about moral issues since *A Survey of Christian Ethics* was written in the middle 1960s and published in 1967. Parts One and Two build upon the motif pattern used before, and readers who are not familiar with the motif patterns developed in the earlier work may find it useful, though not necessary, to examine that treatment. Part Three of this work considers developments that have some continuity with the past but which are now so important to the field as to require separate consideration. Part Four discusses frameworks for doing Christian ethics that have developed in the last fifteen years.

No overview of so complex a field as Christian ethics can ever be complete. Even a month-by-month or quarter-by-quarter summary would miss something. Moreover, bibliographically oriented essays which are prepared close to the appearance of the materials are seldom able to discern thematic developments over a period of several years, which this volume seeks to do.[1]

Because this volume seeks to discern motifs and trends it is selective in its choice of materials. Dominant attention is given to book-length treatments of issues, and the selection of books has been governed by principles of general visibility, but more par-

ticularly by the extent to which any given work illumines the
trend being traced. The chief focus, as in the earlier work, is on
treatments of fundamental stance and theoretical orientation.
Secondary interpretations of the field are not included unless
they make some distinctive contribution of their own, nor are
materials (some in book form and of highest quality) that discuss
from a Christian perspective one or several particular social
issues, such as abortion, affirmative action, civil disobedience,
investment policy, population problems, racism, war-peace concerns, and the like. This very list of issues shows many changes
over what a similar enumeration of burning issues might have
looked like in the middle 1960s and will, undoubtedly, be out-
dated before the last reader has perused this volume.

The limitations resulting from these methodological constraints
are frightening to me as I consider the numerous fine Christian
ethicists whose contributions do not get mentioned. Some of the
most active of these, who address particular issues, who serve as
leaders in our professional guilds, who devote great time and
dedication working on denominational or ecumenical studies, or
whose work appears primarily in journals, will have to take
comfort from the fact that the same criteria applied to the author
of this book would exclude mention of his work.

A Survey of Christian Ethics was intended to be a useful teaching device but also to make a more constructive delineation of a
field than does the usual textbook. For a number of reasons it
does not lend itself to revision in the usual manner, and can
continue to be useful as a report upon a longer and earlier period
than that covered here. There also was a very practical element in
the decision to bring out a new volume. The older work, written
in a time of different sensitivities about language, contains a
number of instances involving the use of the generic male pronoun as a means of speaking about all persons. It would have
been unacceptable to issue a revision of that work without cor-
recting this matter, but to do so would have forced resetting the
entire previous work—not merely adding new sections or chapters. The resulting cost would have exceeded by some multiple
integer the combined cost of leaving the first work in print and
doing a completely new overview.

In the mid-1960s, when I concluded the writing of the first survey, I judged the then current mood of much Christian ethical reflection to be a thrust toward polemical exclusion, and observed that "some literature in contemporary Christian ethics consists more of arguments against rejected alternatives than of defense for what is advocated."[2] I also suggested that the various ways of doing Christian ethics might be utilized together in a "Comprehensive complementarity" in which different motifs function alongside each other. Looking over the developments that have occurred in Christian thinking about ethics in the last fifteen years, one gathers an impression that the tendency to polemical exclusion has waned, particularly with respect to the formulation of norms. Sharp issues now tend to be posed with respect to the implementation of ethical decisions, but even here polemical exclusion is not the all-encompassing pattern. If there is a place where bridges need building and lines of communication need extending it is between the people at work in the three different frameworks discussed in Part Four. The people are separated less by conscious argument than by preoccupation, but that in no way diminishes the benefit that could come from greater interaction.

Thinking about and writing this volume has spanned a period of bereavement is my personal life. The editors of the Oxford University Press, like associates from every neighborly, institutional, and professional contact I have, have been caring and supportive during the period surrounding the sickness and death of my first wife. The editors have also been patient waiting for this to get done—probably the one obligation that was delayed too long. I am deeply grateful for all these expressions of support and patience.

Writing this work in the context of full-time teaching in Christian ethics in a theological setting has driven me to recognize a need to develop my own systematic ethic, and thinking about the framework and content of that is well under way. I have deliberately restrained myself in this volume from indicating in any but a brief fashion how I respond to the many options, but such restraint will not, providence willing, be indefinitely maintained.

Many people have helped directly with the preparation of this volume. Professor Thomas C. Oden read much of the rough draft and gave me the benefit of his judgment about substance and of his marvelous sense of writing style. Dr. John Vincent read most of the draft in a more advanced stage and made some helpful suggestions. Professor Janet Fishburn read several chapters, particularly those about which she is expert and I am still journeyman. Professors Donald G. Jones and Donald K. Swearer each read the chapter about which their grasp of issues is more ample than mine and I benefited from their observations. My gratitude for the collegial support thus shown must be expressed, though each of these persons knows even more particularly than the reader that I have used my own judgment and inclination in shaping the final result.

In writing this volume I have learned one of the advantages of teaching graduate students. They provide a ready cadre of persons able to take draft copy and help turn it into manuscript copy. In the case of this book, Dr. Daniel Ling helped prepare nine of the chapters; the Reverend Pat Stewart, two; and Elaine Minsky and Terrence Rowland, one. After that, Mr. Ronald Hesselgrave examined the manuscript as returned from copy-editing—checking quotes yet another time and finding things needing correction even after all the previous efforts. When the galleys came, Mr. James Speer read them with eyes fresh for that task. All of these undertook the work under constraints in their schedules and pressures on mine. They have convinced me that no word processer will outperform the person, expecially in checking style, structure, and sources. But in preparing this manuscript I have also learned one of the important obligations of teaching in graduate school. It is almost impossible to carve out time that is totally free of interruptions. Ms. Leary Murphy, the faculty administrative aide in the Drew Theological School, has helped me to marshall my time so that I have been able to write as well as provide necessary academic support for students. Finally, I record my gratitude to Drew University, which was a marvelous host to me when I wrote *A Survey of Christian Ethics* and is now a supportive home.

I would repeat here what I wrote a decade and a half ago. "Thinking about moral issues from the perspective of Christian faith should never cease. What has already been done is but prologue to what must yet be undertaken. The world is moving, faith is pilgrimage, and the intellectual enterprise must both report and challenge what transpires. Perhaps this analysis can contribute to ongoing discussion about the Christian understanding of moral responsibility."

Drew Forest   E. L. Long, Jr.
Winter 1982

Contents

I
Norms

1
Broadening Concepts of Moral Deliberation

While some theologians in the long course of Christian moral reflection have rejected the place of reason in making moral judgments, many others have defended the place and significance of a deliberative approach to the formulation of the ethical norm. The defenders of reason have included those who have been impressed by the autonomy of reason and have deferred so extensively to its dictates as to doubt the value or importance of ethical insights that come from faith or from revealed understandings of God's will. Others have simply found the categories of philosophical thought to be useful vehicles for stating Christian imperatives.

The recent tendency among thinkers who accord reasoning a significant place in Christian ethics has been to examine the contributions possible from moral reasoning without mounting a strong contention for the sovereignty of reason or for the autonomy of a rational way of formulating ethical norms. The use of reason has become increasingly functional rather than ideological, honored for suggestive contributions to a broadened process of moral judgment rather than made the basis for an exclusive methodology. Charles Curran has voiced a feeling applicable not only to developments in the Roman Catholic tradition in which he stands but to most recent Protestant thought as well. "Certainly," he writes, "the Church and the individual Christian must use their reason to find out the good, but the knowledge of good and evil goes far beyond a mere cerebral and rationalistic approach."[1]

Assessing the situation in theological ethics in the mid-1960s, James Sellers judged that the revival of theological interest in the previous two or three decades had undercut to some extent the impulse to think comprehensively about moral judgments and to explore the principles and theories that can be reasonably discerned as foundational for moral judgment. "The time has come," he wrote, "for a further effort at systematic thought in Christian ethics, one which can participate in the theological revisions which are modifying neo-orthodoxy, and one which can attempt to make contact with the moral dilemmas of American Society in an effort to encourage ethical thinking."[2]

Proposing an approach that embodies the pragmatic reason of the American temper, Sellers explores the importance for moral judgment of *stance*, of *wisdom*, of *action*, and of *fulfillment*. While he professes to seek a vision of comprehensiveness, he acknowledges that any formulation of a Christian ethic in a particular time or place is bound to be revised with the further unfolding of experience.

Commenting on *stance* as the first focal point—or "locus"—of moral decision making, Sellers contends that since ethics "consists in considered reflection about human actions from the point of view of some critical standards of excellence,"[3] the development of an ethic depends upon the discovery and careful delineation of this standard of judgment—a standard that is just as prior to and formative for faith as the other way around.

> The task of the theological ethicist is always to present the *distinctive* elements of a critical standard of excellence which is to be found in the Christian faith (or, more broadly, the Judaeo-Christian tradition). "Distinctive" as used here is a dual concept. It refers first and most importantly to the vision or expectation for human conduct that is *permanently* peculiar

to the Judaeo-Christian tradition. It refers in the second place to the special insights out of this reservoir which this tradition may deliver anew *in changed times*, or after an epochal crisis, when the Gospel—the promise and reality of wholeness for man—must be retranslated for a new generation, and particular strands of this tradition, not so relevant before, suddenly become of burning importance.[4]

In making this argument, Sellers is wrestling not only with the tension between the permanent and the changing in our perceptions of the critical standard of excellence, but also with the tension between the experience of forgiveness (understood by so many in terms of *sola fide*) and the importance of dedication and achievement in natural human activity. Taking account of the flavor of contemporary human experience, he argues "that on the whole the divine initiative and grace are now more faithfully mediated through the symbols of human initiative (especially at the level of human relations, but not excluding 'muscular effort'), than otherwise."[5] Consequently, we must acknowledge the value of activistic efforts to produce change, without turning our agendas into idolatries.

Discussing the importance of *wisdom*, Sellers acknowledges that Christian ethics owes, and will continue to owe, many of its insights to revelation, but contends that more insight is needed for Christian decision-making than can be garnered from revelation itself.

Christian ethics stands between two sources of insight and is in interdependent relation with each. In primary fashion it is dependent on the conventional sources of and aids to revelation —biblical study and exegesis, church history, and theological reflection. From these it draws the dominating features of its stance and deduces criteria for controlling the uses of non-revelational knowledge. But it is also necessarily dependent on the full range of secular knowledge—"worldly wisdom"—to incarnate the deliverances of revelation and in some ways to supplement, correct, and replace our obsolescent, ideological, and incomplete versions of these deliverances.[6]

Sellers's argument takes all sources of judgment seriously, without making any of them by itself into an absolute. Scripture is acknowledged as a source of guidance, but only insofar as it reveals the gift of wholeness; personal judgment is considered important, but is not (anymore than community judgment) allowed controlling authority; knowledge of technical factors (reliable data from the natural and social sciences as well as awareness of the dynamics in any particular social situation) is judged to be indispensable but not singularly decisive. Any ethic suitable for our time will weave together the signals from each of these several sources of guidance into a wise perception of a contemporary imperative. Reasoning becomes more than a process of deducing right directions for action from first principles. It is a process of perceiving some critical standard of excellence, with great sensitivity to all the factors that make that standard worth honoring.

Sellers suggests that *action* is important for Christian ethics because we get to the heart of the ethical enterprise only insofar as we use wisdom to understand what persons should do as agents. The attempt to act ethically reveals a gap between the divine norm and human conduct—a gap put forth in uncompromising (and therefore unhelpful) terms by divine-command theologies and overlooked or explicitly downplayed in "softer" versions of the Social Gospel. While Roman Catholic moral theology, situation ethics, and middle axiom approaches to doing Christian ethics all attempt to mediate this gap, they succeed only to the extent that they redefine the norm as a human and divine reality and adopt a complementarity between the concepts of promise and fulfillment to replace the dichotomy between love and justice made so central in much neo-orthodox reflection. Among the possibilities opened by this approach is the chance to attach importance to relationships that can be described as *friendly* rather than either as fully loving or merely just.

In a subsequent extensive work Sellers elaborates the meaning of action into a concept of *public ethics*. The doing of ethics becomes far more than the study of the theoretical grounds for deciding norms—far more than a quasi-scholarly debate about the relative place of ideals, rules, or situations as beginning points for moral judgments. Ethics becomes an examination of the public ethos—including the manners and mores of the society—and is likely to be viable only in relation to some struggle to deal with large public issues. In a consideration of the views of Fletcher, Ramsey and others, Sellers offers a broadened view of *agape*, of rules, and of situations. He argues that agape cannot become the main category of Christian discipleship, replacing the reception of the benefits of Christ as proclaimed in the Gospel. The Gospel is concerned with indicating how life is renewed in terms of the future, and is therefore inevitably teleological. Consequently, the Christian ethicist must discern the movement of public meaning taking place at any particular time or in any circumstance.

One has only to look at the contemporary revolution in human values, involving such moral fields as civil rights, economic dignity, and the big-power consensus against nuclear war, the equality of women, or the cruelty of capital punishment, to see that some rules, at least, do change, and possibly for the better. It is the business of the theologian or public ethicist to delineate the criteria for appraising and governing these changes and for connecting them with man's pilgrimage.[7]

The focus of concern should be not only on the dynamic of the Gospel, rather than the ideal of agape, but also on the moral tradition that constitutes the ethos out of which the community of faith engenders rules or changes rules as circumstances operate. Failure to understand that ethos, to discern its contours and reflect about it critically, will tempt an ethicist to ignore the very factors most determinative in public responses. Finally, a more discerning understanding of situations will emerge from a process of looking, not at the particulars of an isolated decisional moment, but at the whole complex of circumstances (both temporal and geographic) in relation to which one must act. "The situation is thus one's history and his space and his engagement with others in his community. It is his 'world.' It is his greater community with its own peculiar pilgrimage, tradition, memory of crises, and sets of rules that have kept men on the right road in the past."[8] Such a critical analysis and reflective judgment about situations is far more akin to deliberation than reading signals from immediate contexts.

The fourth focus of a theological ethic is *fulfillment*. Sellers examines both the ultimate dimensions of fulfillment (as they would be embodied in redemption) and proximate dimensions (as they would be realized in sanctification). Fulfillment involves overcoming three conditions that beset human beings. Only as we are aware that we are finite will we cope with the fact that all our actions are inadequate; only as we become aware of our tendency to provincialism and our underachieving will we passionately seek the accomplishments that can meet the claims of others; only as we acknowledge our fallen condition can we overcome the self-deception that furnishes a false confidence or results in a lost vision. Sanctification is a necessary correlate to eschatology, and we must talk about human fulfillment by reasoning "forward from sanctification" as well as by reasoning "backward from salvation."

In developing his approach to moral reasoning, Sellers utilizes a great deal of cultural diagnosis, stressing the ways in which the social, intellectual, and cultural ethos affects the judgments that come out of it. Arthur J. Dyck draws his understanding of moral reasoning out of the unique experiences of professional practice. He has taught on faculties of arts and sciences and in professional schools of public health, theology, and military leadership and has made a determined effort to build lines of communication between Christian moral reflection and general moral reasoning. This effort, born not merely of the teaching situations in which Dyck has found himself but of a deliberate conviction that ethical reasoning has a validity of its own, has much to contribute to theological reflection about moral matters.

Dyck is strongly convinced that normative considerations are central to the ethical agenda, even though such normative considerations must take circumstances into account. "Ethics" he writes, "asks about what is right or good or virtuous; it seeks also to identify and characterize moral arguments, and to investigate whether and the extent to which these arguments, or

the decisions they are intended to justify, are rationally warranted."[9] Dyck considers and rejects the position, which he finds
represented by Paul Lehmann, that the only correct approach to
doing Christian ethics is to ground the discernment of the good
in a special community of faith. He rejects as well the contention,
which he finds exemplified by William Frankena, that the nature
of the good can be known philosophically and with recourse
only to philosophical considerations. Dyck also rejects dualistic
schemes in which Christian ethics and philosophical ethics are
taken to be distinct, yet complementary, sources of normative
judgment. Dyck considers ethics to be an independent inquiry
which uses philosophical, religious, and professional inputs without becoming subservient to any of them. The importance of
ethical reflection is to avoid moral tragedy, that is, the realization
after the fact that, had a person reflected carefully upon a
particular course of action, she or he would have made a different
decision.

Dyck is dissatisfied with a strictly utilitarian foundation for
ethics. He cites as contravening evidence the basic attitude
governing medical practice that the needs of the patient, not a
calculus of survival, are the touchstone of therapy. Physicians, he
observes, "have promises to keep and commitments to honor,
and it would be considered a grave breach of ethics to adopt as a
working policy the attitude that one's patients ought to be risked,
sacrificed, or abandoned wherever by doing so a greater good
can be accomplished."[10]

Dyck's concern with the inherent claim of certain actions is
based upon arguments he credits to W. David Ross. The keeping
of promises, the restraining of impulses to redress past wrongs
vindictively, and the showing of gratitude are examples of actions
that make inherent claims. Dyck explores the distinction made
by Paul Taylor and others between act utilitarianism and rule
utilitarianism and concludes that to take utility as rationally self-
evident is a formalistic rather than a utilitarian judgment. Dyck
feels that certain rules would make a moral claim even if social
existence were not dependent upon the development of such
rules and allegiance to them. Rules have a formal claim and are to
be respected because of that claim.

For Dyck, one of the central ingredients in Christian ethics—
the ideal of love for the neighbor—involves both beneficence
(which can be justified on utilitarian grounds) and the principle
of non-maleficence (which cannot necessarily be so justified).
Finding in the Mosaic covenant an unambiguous (formalistic)
obligation to protect life, Dyck extends the notion of inherently
defined wrongs to include stealing and adultery. Dyck also notes
that the Mosaic covenant specifies not only the nature of certain
acts that are prohibited because considered inherently wrong, but
rules of conduct for society which preclude the performance of
those actions. He chides philosophers for ignoring these social
mandates and declares:

> . . . it is not enough to know what is right-making and
> wrong-making at the level of moral principles. The human
> associations that make it possible to know what is right and
> wrong, to conform to what is right, and to avoid what is evil,
> need also to be identified so that the actions that would be
> destructive of them can be identified as morally wrong-
> making.[11]

The consequence of Dyck's position is not to make it impossible to take circumstances into account when deciding what
to do, but to render it illegitimate to abrogate the normative
judgment in order to respond to circumstances. The epitome of
the ethical person becomes "an ideal moral judge" who weighs
instances of doubt and conflict with disinterested care while
taking due account of the normative ingredients that must be
factored into the analysis of every situation.[12] By studying how
such an ideal moral judge would defend the judgments rendered
in such a process of deliberation, we have a clue to the nature of
moral reflection. "We come to understand what we mean by
terms like *right* when we come to identify the processes by
which we would try to convince ourselves or others that what
we say is right is in fact right."[13] For Dyck the ability to be an
ideal moral observer depends both upon qualities of the judge
and the conditions under which the judge deliberates. Disinterestedness and dispassionateness depend not only upon the qualities brought to decisions by the individual making them but

also upon structural safeguards that remove the agent from too close an interest in the outcome, and that permit all affected groups to have a functional voice in the decision.

In his book *Three Issues in Ethics*, John Macquarrie looks at the issues facing theological ethicists at the beginning of the 1970s. He rejects efforts to do ethics either wholly by formulating rules or wholly by responding to situations. This forces him to advance a deliberative approach that depends upon moral reasoning in a broad sense. Searching for a point of contact between Christian morality and other ethical systems and for a kind of theological approach that can engender and sustain that contact, Macquarrie makes his starting point the concern for what it means to be human. He rejects those approaches that deal with this question in exclusively Christocentric terms and moves instead to a natural law approach that develops principles of conduct in accord with human nature. For Macquarrie, the idea of natural law should be wrested from the static essentialistic framework in which it has been traditionally couched and re-formulated in dynamic terms. Natural law must not be based upon considerations of the merely natural order of things, but upon a broader framework of insights and meanings drawn from the whole scope of experience. Hence, the idea of natural law "refers to a norm of responsible conduct, and suggests a kind of fundamental guideline or criterion that comes before all rules or particular formulations of law."[14]

Natural law as Macquarrie reconceives it provides a valid way to link religion with morality. Macquarrie is opposed to the subordination of either to the other. He finds the reality of the fundamental human experience evidenced in the fact that people will indeed appeal to a "natural justice" when facing and observing wrong. They will do so from a variety of stances, some theological, others merely ontological or metaphysical. Macquarrie makes human thinking and moral reasoning crucial to the doing of ethics. Reiterating the distinction between natural law and any particular rules or precepts, Macquarrie contends that natural law cannot be reduced to mere prescription, and thus "is not so much itself a 'law' as rather a touchstone for determining the justice or morality of actual laws and rules."[15] Like Dyck,

Macquarrie refers to Sir David Ross's concept of prima facie duties, which he feels express a "fundamental moral knowledge, given with experience itself" which is shared by Christians and non-Christians and provides a basis for cooperation between them.

Taking into account the increasing complexity of moral choice and the erosion of traditional sources of moral judgment, J. Philip Wogaman has developed an approach to making moral judgments, which he consciously presents as an alternative to situation ethics (which he thinks collapses into the moral relativism of our time), and two forms of resurgent interest in the enunciation of norms. Unwilling to adopt the middle-axiom approach of John C. Bennett[16] or the re-emphasis on rules of Paul Ramsey,[17] Wogaman suggests a methodology that is tentative about particular judgments while remaining faithful to the central affirmation of Christian faith.

The heart of Wogaman's approach is the concept of methodological presumption. Unlike situationalism or calculative realism, this approach takes into account commitment to particular norms but, unlike evangelical perfectionism, does not hold that such norms can be fully embodied in action. Norms create a presumption that certain actions are mandated unless a distinct case can be made for a different judgment. Wogaman suggests that each of us has initial presumptions that operate in our thinking unless they are deliberately challenged. We place a conscious or unconscious burden of proof more against certain actions than against others. These presumptions may be based on procedural, principled, ideological, or empirical sources of judgment.

The task of the Christian ethicist is to ask what presumptions are most compatible with Christian faith—recognizing that not all presumptions enjoy universal assent, even among Christians. Wogaman holds that belief in a personal God is important; and that the knowledge of God as made known in the life, death, and resurrection of Christ is a special element in a Christian approach. The doctrine of creation is helpful because it helps us to understand how God is related to the structures and events of the world. Other positive presumptions include the goodness of creation, the value of individual life and the right of individuals to be free, the unity of the human family in God, and the equality of persons in relationship to God. The negative presumptions, which acknowledge the fact that limitations are built into the human condition, include a recognition of human finitude and a realization of human sinfulness. Moral choices and social policies that ignore the weight of the positive presumptions or the counterweight of the negative presumptions bear a heavy burden of proof as to their legitimacy.

These moral presumptions are not the final source of judgment. While Wogaman carefully states and sympathetically considers the position of those who seek inflexible and unexceptionable mandates for obedience, he finally rejects their position in favor of the view that deviation from norms is possible (and sometimes morally required) but stands under a great burden of proof. The balancing, weighing, and comparing of options which Wogaman sees to be at the heart of moral decision-making is underscored in a chapter which shows that certain values are found only in polar relationship to other values. Among the polar presumptions that Wogaman enumerates are the individual/social nature of man; the interplay of freedom/responsibility; the contrast of subsidiarity/universality; the importance of conservation/innovation (continuity versus change) in the social process; and optimism/pessimism. The last contrast is perhaps not strictly moral but does have a bearing upon our approach to making moral decisions. These polar presumptions identify the boundaries within which judgments must lie. For instance, in any social system,

> We know that there must be some freedom and some responsibility. This judgment has great force where freedom has been crushed or responsibility is openly mocked. But the polar presumption cannot by itself tell us in a given situation how to relate the two; it can only say that neither should be excluded. Where either seems excluded, a burden of proof must be met.[18]

Wogaman discusses the influence of groups upon the making of decisions, of fundamental world-views (ideologies) upon our perceptions of reality, and the difficulties of translating moral judgments into concrete social actions. The result is an illuminating discussion of the necessity for comprehensive moral reasoning—a reasoning not uninformed by normative criteria, yet astutely aware of the need to assess the appropriateness of those criteria in the circumstances of their application.

Bio-medical ethics, which is one form of the vocational ethics with which Chapter X is specifically concerned, frequently proceeds by discussing problems and cases. But any discussion of problems and cases raises issues about the grounds upon which they are to be analyzed. Tom L. Beauchamp and James F. Childress have examined the principles that apply to the discussion of bio-medical problems. In doing so they have developed a deliberative treatment of moral reasoning that, like the work of Arthur Dyck, utilizes W. D. Ross's prima facie categories and pushes for normative rigor, and, like the work of Philip Wogaman, uses the idea of burden of proof for dealing with situations according to the principles. In the resulting analysis the role of principles is examined with attention to several theoretical problems in ethical theory.

For Beauchamp and Childress, moral deliberation is a process by which the deciding agent tries to justify certain actions in an effort to systematize and clarify terms that too often float undefined or inadequately defined in an atmosphere of ethical discourse. Accordingly, the authors differentiate ethical theories, principles, rules, and particular judgments or action.

> A *judgment* is a decision, verdict, or conclusion about a particular action. Although the precise nature of the distinction between rules and principles is somewhat controversial, *rules* state that action of a certain kind ought (or ought not) to be done because they are right (or wrong). A simple example is, "It is wrong to lie to a patient." *Principles* are more general and fundamental than moral rules and serve as their foundation. The principle of respect for persons, for example, may ground several moral rules of the "it is wrong to lie" sort. Finally, *theories* are bodies of principles and rules, more or less systematically related. They include second-order principles and rules about what to do when there are conflicts.[19]

Ethical reflection involves all these elements. Professional codes, for instance, may appear as rules but they also rest on principles and guide practice. They even raise issues of theory, once the necessary task of justifying them is undertaken.

Four principles are examined which have received repeated expression in traditional philosophy—autonomy, or the belief that persons are to be responsible for (and to be respected as capable of) their own decisions; the principle of non-maleficence, or the maxim that one is not to inflict harm or allow injury to occur; the principle of beneficence, which requires us to contribute to the health and welfare of others; and the principle of justice, which in its distributive form guides the allocation of benefits under conditions of necessary limitation, and in its commutative form suggests proper behavior between persons (such as truth-telling). The authors examine a whole series of medical practices that can be analyzed in terms of the principles, and while the understanding of the problems themselves gains much from the discussion, the normative process is clearly central. For Beauchamp and Childress, "ethics as the systematic examination of the moral life is designed to illuminate what we ought to do by asking us to consider and reconsider our ordinary actions, judgments, and justifications."[20] Such consideration, and reconsideration, depends for its fruitfulness upon principles of generalization and the rules derived from them. The result, which utilizes deliberation without polemical exclusion, clearly deserves to be classified as a broadened concept of moral reasoning.

The broad uses of reason portrayed in this chapter are not without precedents and parallels in the Christian tradition. Indeed, if there is an aberration, it is in those forms of theology that, under the pressure of the Enlightenment sought to make reason autonomous. The claims for the sovereignty of reason that were made in the late nineteenth and early twentieth century have tended to wane in recent years. Perhaps James Gustafson is particularly insightful in downplaying the terms *reason* and *deliberation* and speaking extensively about discernment. His concept of discernment involves moral reasoning in a broad sense that includes empathy, appreciation, imagination, and sensitivity in approaching issues. It connotes the wise exercise of moral judgment and depends upon experience, a set of first principles and the capacity to reflect critically about their application, awareness of situational factors and the ability to sense their implications, emotive and aesthetic sensibilities, and the ability to weigh different claims.

> The discerning act of moral discernment is impossible to program and difficult to describe. It involves perceptivity, discrimination, subtlety, sensitivity, clarity, rationality, and accuracy. And while some men seem to have it as a "gift of the gods," others achieve it by experience and training, by learning and acting. It is probably more akin to the combination of elements that go into good literary criticism and good literary creativity than it is to the combination of elements that make a good mathematician or logician; it is both rational and affective.[21]

While human processes of discernment in the Christian life are no different than those same processes in the lives of other persons, the inputs can be different and broader: self-offering to God in prayer and in worship, contemplation of the world as a created order under providential concern, different loci of trust and confidence, and the contemplation of values especially honored in the Christian tradition—all engender important sensibilities. Rules and principles also have a place, subject to careful, sensitive, appreciation. Discernment exists in continuity with the past. It acknowledges the role and function of law but the need to read law in light of circumstances. It has many similarities with the virtue of prudence. Reason and intellectual discrimination are uppermost, but gifts of the spirit, including love, trust, and hope, are also crucial.

Gustafson's ethics often begins with a consideration of human experience in general. He is deeply concerned to see continuities between the moral experience of humanity in general and that experience as it relates to the special dimensions of the Christian life. His analysis utilizes both philosophical and social scientific insights without adopting the specialized jargon of either, but it does not preclude careful attention to and appropriation of specifically theological insights from the Christian tradition. Every issue is a subject for analysis. Such deft handling of complexities, without polemical exclusion or plumping for one formulation, makes Gustafson's approach a model of a broadening conceptualization of moral reasoning.

Since Kant, many philosophers have stressed autonomy in moral reasoning in ways that consider it most valid when free from extrinsic measures of legitimacy, particularly when free from religiously imposed canons of judgment. The thought of Newman Smyth illustrates how completely some theological ethicists made Christian ethics subservient to philosophical judgments.[22] One of the interesting efforts to move in the opposite direction is Keith Ward's *Ethics and Christianity*.[23] This philosophical work contends that a Christian way of reasoning about morals has special features that are objective in content, attitudinal in the insistence that the true moral demand is embodied in Jesus Christ, charismatic in its view that forgiveness must reconstitute the self before the spirit can do its work, and teleological in holding to the belief that morality is functional in relation to a final fulfillment of the person. Instead of requiring Christian ethics to meet the tests of an autonomous reason, Ward contends that philosophical ethics must meet the tests of Christian understanding.

It does not necessarily broaden the concept of reason to argue for its autonomy, nor does it necessarily narrow it to contend that Christian faith provides certain frameworks for moral thinking. The concept of reason is broadened when its dynamics are examined, when ambiguity and uncertainty in its contributions are allowed for, when its use is taken as important along with other sources of judgment, and when it is pursued in conjunction with other ways of formulating the ethical norm.

2

Enlarging Concepts of Law and New Appreciation of Rules

This chapter surveys a group of writings which deals either with law or with rules as important to Christian ethics. Its logical arrangement, not intended to suggest chronological development, moves from discussions of law that are practically forms of moral deliberation to discussions of law (or of rules) that are strongly prescriptive.

The concern that ethics includes normative content is not necessarily confined to a deliberative approach which engages in moral reasoning. An equally important way of stressing the normative element is to delineate specific actions deemed to be inherently right. Unfortunately, the term *principles* comes into use in both these ways of underscoring the normative element in ethics. But principles that stress the reason as a source of ethical judgment and principles that merely generalize the content of mandated obligation are different types of ethical norms.

Similarly, contrasting meanings can be attached to the word *law*. It can mean a body of specific declarations concerning right and wrong and the resolve to enforce those declarations by extrinsic authority. On the other hand, law can denote a process of dealing with the varieties of human interaction with structural fairness and by a wise adjudication of conflicting claims. In keeping with this second concept, Harold Berman defines law as "the process of resolving conflicts and creating channels of co-operation by allocation of rights and duties. . . ."[1] Speaking of a prevalent theological tendency to make law and love contrasting rubrics, Berman argues that such a simplistic anti-legalism

> . . . misconceives the function of legal rules. Rules are not a denial of our unique, individual personalities. On the contrary, they are necessary to protect our unique, individual personalities from capricious, arbitrary, and oppressive action. It is true, of course, that they are cast in terms of similarities among people; they treat people as members of classes or categories. They must do so in order to preserve the basic principle of law, that like cases should be decided alike. But this is not only a principle of justice; it is also a principle of love. For it is not love to treat a person unequally with others in a situation in which he ought to be treated equally. It would not be love for a legislature or a court or administrative body to require some persons to pay higher taxes, for example, than others living in exactly the same circumstances. It may well be love for a person to give his property to another person who has greater need of it, but it would not be love for society to permit that other person to take the property without permission. Living, as we do, a common life of interaction with each other, our personalities require—for love's sake—the protection of general principles impartially administered.[2]

In wrestling with the normative element in Christian ethics, Walter Muelder identifies three types of moral law. One type consists of positive prescription and is expressed in codes having authoritative sanction. Muelder is not attracted to this kind of law. Another type of moral law is defended by appeals to reason but embodies the convictions of particular groups. Such "natural law" gives birth to particular formulations, which take on prescriptive qualities. Muelder is not advocating this approach any more than the first. The third type of moral law, the one of particular interest to Muelder, "presents one or more values as ultimate norms or demands."[3] All decisions, however much they take circumstances and situations into account (as they certainly ought to do), are to be judged by their consistency with principles that guide moral action. These principles are "normative laws of choice"[4] for making disciplined and coherent decisions at logical, axiological, personalistic, and communitarian levels.

Law, for Muelder, is a set of governing directions for proper moral reasoning. The moral situation is described as follows:

> From the standpoint of the actor a moral situation involves the following: (1) examining and clarifying the alternatives from which to choose; (2) elaborating rationally the consequences of the alternatives; (3) projecting the self imaginatively into the predicted situation, that is, making a dramatic identification of the present self with the future self in the envisaged situation; (4) identifying the self imaginatively with the points of view of those persons whom the proposed act will most seriously affect; (5) estimating and comparing the values involved in each of the projected consequential situations and comparing these situations; (6) deciding; and (7) acting.[5]

Drawing upon eleven formulations developed by E. S. Brightman and three added by L. Harold DeWolfe, Muelder enunciates fourteen formal principles (or "laws") that ensure the cogency of moral reasoning. Two of the laws are purely *formal*, have to do with the will alone, and state norms that must be honored if the moral will is to act rationally. They stress the importance of logical consistency and the obligation to pursue the ideals a person professes. The six laws of the second group are *axiological*, and indicate the principles to which the values willed by a moral agent ought to conform. Consistency and coherence are expected; consequences are to be taken into account; the will is to seek the best possible values in each situation and to develop values that are specifically relevant to a situation. The widest range of values is to be realized and empirical values are to be controlled by ideals. A third group of laws is *personalistic* and points to the desired effect of conduct upon individuals. One law stresses the importance of each person realizing the maximum value possible consistent with moral law; another suggests that each person is to respect others and treat them as ends in themselves; and a third points to the importance of an ideal concept of what the whole personality should be, both individually and socially. A fourth group of laws is *communitarian* and points to the social context in which choice is made. One of these laws stresses the importance of cooperation; another, the importance of each person serving the best interest of the group; and a third, the importance of having an ideal of what the community ought to become.

Muelder points out that these laws "are derived by analyzing all the principal aspects of moral situations and the moral life and then formulating the universal principles which comprise a coherent unity."[6] They comprise a rational system and are valid in any cultural context. All ethicists, including situationalists, either consciously or unconsciously appeal to these considerations in vindicating their approach. Muelder stresses the value of respecting the principle of autonomy in Christian ethics since "no ideal or belief is morally binding until it has been acknowledged and self-imposed."[7] He contends that the search for coherence is common to all ethical reflection, but that whereas Christocentric ethicists like Barth, Ramsey, and Lehmann demand that such coherence be with Jesus Christ, his approach is based on the belief "that as an interdisciplinary field Christian social ethics should be coherent scientifically, philosophically, and theologically, no one discipline dictating the coherence."[8] Clearly, he uses the rubric of law to expound a view of moral reasoning practically synonymous with those examined in the previous chapter.

Bernard Häring's reconceptualization of Roman Catholic moral theology in his three-volume work *The Law of Christ* has been an enormous influence upon the thinking about Christian morality. That influence began to be felt early in the 1960s and permeated American theological reflection more fully after the translations of the work were completed in 1966.[9] Häring's judgment that the natural law tradition has become too much a "rigidly rationalistic ethic of essences"[10] was an exciting one, coming as it did before Vatican II.

His treatment of norm and law in the first volume develops a broad view of law as that which serves human values and expounds the spiritual "law of Christ" as a basis for an obedience in which grace is given central importance without abrogating obligation. The "law of Christ" means liberty—liberty because it is connected with grace, and because it transcends the reductionism of rigid prescription. Granting that human laws are sometimes oppressive, Häring, in a formulation strikingly similar to Berman's, declares: "But human law is not merely a cross; in its inner sense it is the way to justice, a support of weakness, a fulfillment of the order of the divine wisdom, a work of love through community and for community."[11]

A footnote in volume three of *The Law of Christ* is highly instructive. Explaining a distinction he draws in the text between the "modest minimum" which may legitimately be imposed, even with external sanction, as part of the moral obligation, and the far more extensive possibilities of the inner law, Häring disassociates himself in the supplemental commentary both from those Roman Catholics who develop too great an "aversion for a hyperjuridical type of moral theology found in certain manuals" (to the extent that such an aversion leads to the theoretical denial of a place for prescription) and from evangelical theologians (who have no theoretical apparatus for relating law and liberty). Appreciation for liberty cannot consist merely of aversion to law. He contends that "we are concerned indeed with the reverence for the ordinances of the Creator. We are solicitous for the discernment of spirits which the external commandment of God serves. But beyond all this we are also determined to defend the true liberty of the children of God; saying *Yes* to the clearly recognized prescriptive commandments is prerequisite to the ascent to loftier heights."[12]

More recently, Häring has returned to the task of creating a comprehensive exposition of moral theology, a summary treatment reflecting the influence of changes that have so rocked the theological world—not least the Catholic Church—in the past several years. The title of his new interpretation *Free and Faithful in Christ* may reflect liberation terminology, but its argument is a revised version of the earlier work rather than an utterly new way of dealing with the issues. The stress Häring places on freedom is balanced by a corresponding emphasis on faithfulness to Christ. "We cannot choose one or the other," he writes, "we can only have both together in their creativeness. Either we make a conscientious and solidary option for creative liberty and fidelity or we lose sight of continuity of life and thus become vulnerable to all kinds of manipulation."[13] Häring suggests that norms can be expressed on three levels. The lowest level is the expressive, evocative, level of guidance. A second level is more truly moral and involves the discerning of proper uses for norms and rules—a discerning that takes into account the historical context in which principle, norms, or rules are considered. Like Muelder, Häring argues that norms are important and that even the proponents of the "new morality" actually utilize norms and suggest rules—though the rules which Häring has in mind are somewhat more like rules or codes than the norms of which Muelder speaks. The cumulative experience of our obedience (both individual and corporate) is an important source of normative judgment, argues Häring, but must be filtered by contemporary judgment because old rules may become more self-serving than functional to the public good. Deontological imperatives must be weighed in light of teleological considerations because a rule is valid only if it serves an appointed purpose of making life more loving as judged by Jesus Christ.

Häring acknowledges the insight of the situationalist that love is more ultimate than law, and he criticizes the school of thinking (supported by a part of the hierarchy) that overstresses handbook norms; he examines how the relationship between law and liberty has been understood in the Reformation and in subsequent Protestant traditions; he acknowledges the importance of casuistry as a means of taking cases into account; he contends that both legalism and situationalism are inadequate (especially in their insistence on one approach) and declares

> The creative freedom for which Christ has set us free is able and ready to commit itself to a covenant morality; and this includes those norms and rules that guarantee reliability. On the other hand, the demand for absolute obedience and the multiplication of absolute norms is a necessary weapon in the arsenal of authoritarians. Therefore, we must be on guard. Absolutes can be accepted only to the extent that they can be shown not to overlap or to lead to hurtful conflicts.[14]

Charles Curran, whose scholarly odyssey has included long and appreciative association with Häring, has published a number of volumes, several of which consist of essays that look at the fundamental issues of moral theology in terms of specific problems. Curran has done much in his own way to help us to see the necessity of transition in our understanding of natural law and the need to read it in terms of current historical conditions. He has observed that the deontological and teleological models have increasingly given way to a relational/responsibility model—not least in the writing of Häring. He feels that the position Häring develops in *The Law of Christ*, for all its break from the legalism of past Roman Catholic moral theology, still reflects the deontological framework. But Curran also observes that in some later works (though he does not include *Free and Faithful in Christ* in this judgment) Häring changes his language from the deontological to the relational/responsibility model.[15]

In the course of his writings, Curran has been mainly concerned to report the state of this discipline—mainly, but by no means solely, with respect to Roman Catholic discussions. He does so with careful fidelity, and his discussions will be helpful to readers who want the issues of this chapter more fully spelled out with respect to Roman Catholic thinking.[16] Curran does not shy away from the bold conclusion that "the concept of natural law as a deductive methodology based on eternal and immutable essences and resulting in specific absolute norms is no longer acceptable to the majority of Catholic moral theologians writing today."[17] It is one thing, however, to mount a polemic against law that altogether denies the significance of norms, and another to modify (as both Häring and Curran do) the rigidities of the older schemes without abrogating their positive contribution.

Paul Ramsey has examined these matters in his book *Deeds and Rules in Christian Ethics*.[18] Judged both by the number of times this book is mentioned by subsequent writers and the degree to which its terminology has been adopted, it is of pivotal importance. The interest shown by Ramsey in rules is significant, for Ramsey's orientation during the early part of his career was highly deliberative and in his *Basic Christian Ethics* code morality is criticized, Jesus is held to overcome the law, and a long section is devoted to the question "What the Christian Does Without a Code."[19] There are some disadvantages to first publishing one's systematic ethic and then entering the lists of controversy, but Ramsey has not let his early position inhibit him. As a controversialist he may be without peer, and he has been increasingly articulate about the importance of a more normative ethic—an ethic that finds guidance in agape beyond either the concept of duty in deontology or the pursuit of ideal goals in teleology.

Adopting terminology suggested by William Frankena,[20] Ramsey considers two views of how Christian love expresses itself in practice. According to one, called *act-agapism*, the Christian is to deal with each particular situation by assessing the facts of the case and deciding the most loving course of action possible within it. In contrast, *rule-agapism* asks which rules of action most embody the demands of love and seeks to analyze particular circumstances in light of guidance from prior and independently articulated norms. This contrast between two kinds of agapism relates to the debate between normative moralities (whether deliberative or prescriptive) and relational ethics (particularly its situational forms). Ramsey is concerned about certain consequences that flow from situational approaches. (The first essay is a criticism of the essay by a group of British Friends entitled *Toward a Quaker View of Sex* which Ramsey accuses of flinching from the normative declaration to which many of its observations should have led.)

Ramsey acknowledges that the use of the term "rules" is not without its difficulties—difficulties which he locates more on semantic and emotive levels than on a substantive one. He holds no special brief for the terminology he suggests (which he adopted from Frankena) and would be content with a number of alternatives including "'principle,' 'middle axiom,' 'ideal,' 'directive,' 'guidance,' 'orders,' 'ordinances,' the 'structures' of *agape* or of *koinonia* life, the 'style' of the Christian life, or the 'anatomy' or 'pattern' of Christian responsibility."[21] Ramsey certainly cannot be faulted for the ease with which he suggests these alternatives (he omits *laws* or *precepts*) since all these terms have normative implications even though many of them are used in both a deliberative manner and a prescriptive manner.

Ramsey's treatment indicates that he is moving from the deliberative stance to a more prescriptive one in order to underscore the role of the normative in Christian decision-making. Not that Ramsey excludes concern for circumstances—only the contention that circumstances by themselves provide the conditions for determining what love requires. In summary, Ramsey would show that

> . . . a proper understanding of the moral life will be one in which Christians determine what we ought to do in very great measure by determining which rules of action are most love-embodying, but that there are also always situations in which we are to tell what we should do by getting clear about the facts of that situation and then asking what is the loving or the most loving thing to do in it. The latter may even be at work in every case of the creative casuistry of in-principled love going into action. But it will be an instance of thoughtlessness or sentimentality if any Christian in the conduct of his life or any theologian in the doing of Christian ethics seeks to overleap or avoid his responsibility for determining whether there are any love-embodying rules of action, and what these rules may be.[22]

To read Ramsey's book is to be introduced, albeit through the eyes of a critic, to the best-known statements of relational contextualism current in the mid-1960s. In addition to the analysis of the Quaker document on sex which opens the book, Ramsey looks at the thought of John A. T. Robinson and argues that his "new morality" has far more *rule-agapism* in its formulations than the profession of pure *act-agapism* would account for. Examining Paul Lehmann's *act-koinonia* ethics, he finds a consistent refusal (which contrasts with aspects of Barth's thought) to admit a normative aspect to ethics and drums Lehmann, not for his inconsistency but for the inadequacy of his formulations. Considering an essay[23] published by William K. Frankena in

which the categories first suggested in the book *Ethics* are modified, Ramsey commends again the cogency of Frankena's categories and suggests that Frankena is too prone to lean toward the
association of agapism with utilitarian schemes (thus favoring
teleological formulations) and that he should give special attention
to recognizing the importance of deontological elements as well.
He complains that Frankena's definition of pure *rule-agapism* is
too rigid, and equates it with loveless legalism. In contrast,
Ramsey suggests that Christians can embrace specific rules as
well as summary rules in ways that indicate what love requires.

Ramsey expanded and updated the Scottish version of his
book for an American audience and added three essays. One of
these stresses the claim of the general practice over specific circumstances. *Rule-agapism*, in contrast to *act-agapism*, "may entail
or often entails doing what love requires *as a social practice* or as a
rule of practice even when this may not accord with what love
requires in a particular deed."[24] Exceptions to rules are to be
allowed in a careful calculative casuistry, judiciously applied, but
not by simply wiping away the rule by appealing to love.

> If there are any Christian moral or social practices, there cannot
> be exceptions that depart from them by direct general appeals
> to *agape* overriding the rules in particular cases in which the
> agent does not take the weighty responsibility of criticizing
> the practice as a whole and attempting to replace it with
> another. *Agape* justifies no exception within a practice. One
> must rather undertake to reform the accepted practice as a
> whole in some fundamental respect which, he ventures to say,
> would render it generally a more loving practice.[25]

In an extended treatment of Joseph Fletcher, Ramsey finds
him guilty of both arguing for a pure *act-agapism* (even though
professing a middle way between legalism and antinomianism)
and invoking equivalents of general rules. Ramsey's charges are
buttressed by a lengthy detailed examination of Fletcher's works
and conclude with a plea for bringing order and solidity to the
doing of Christian ethics by taking seriously both Roman Catholic

and philosophical discussions. A final essay is a tongue-in-cheek "Letter to John of Patmos from a Proponent of 'The New Morality.'" The reader will have to make his own deductions about the undertaking.

The movement toward increased prescription, represented by Ramsey, moves into possible conversational distance with a movement away from unmitigated prescription on the part of some conservative Protestant moralists. John Murray once said that Christian morality consists of "the meticulous observance of the commandments of God in the minutial details of their prescription."[26] Today, a conservative Christian ethicist, Milton L. Rudnick, wanting to re-emphasize the importance of general standards of right and wrong without inviting the designation legalist, prefers to describe himself as a "rules-deontologist with a contextualist bent."[27] Such a position holds that attention to the future consequences of an act (teleological concerns) and considerations of present circumstances (contextualist concerns) are secondary to the direction sought from "divinely revealed and universally binding principles of conduct."[28] In the development of this position the distinction between rules and principles, while explicitly recognized, tends to blur. Rules are practical and concrete, principles are more general and comprehensive, but both have a function in an evangelical ethic. In determining what Scripture says on a subject, a more primitive and practical concept of the model or pattern is useful. Revelation includes the description of ethical duties in detailed specifics.

> God has not remained silent about the kind of people He wants us to be. He has expressed Himself clearly on this subject, not only by word but also by deed and example. He has given us a vision of Christian personhood. He has conveyed a *sense,* an impression, of how we are to think, feel and act.
>
> The directions or norms that He has given us are more like the counsel and example of a parent than, for example, like a tough set of laws given by a dictator to his subjects. These directions describe concretely the kind of persons we can and should be. They are far more than an abstract set of moral principles, rules, or virtues.[29]

Professor Rudnick characterizes the Ten Commandments as "specific and concrete explanations of what it means to be loving in a variety of relationships and circumstances."[30] The function of biblical norms is to describe and prescribe what love will do.

Norman L. Geisler also advocates a deontological emphasis on norms and underscores the duty "to do what is inherently right apart from the foreseeable consequences."[31] He uses terms like principles, norms, and rules almost interchangeably and stresses their crucial importance for giving ethics a normative foundation. In arguing for the importance of norms he dismisses, as unsatisfactory, antinomianism (which holds there are no norms), generalism (which considers norms to be only generally and not universally binding), and situationalism (which believes there is only one universally binding norm that has to be applied in light of circumstance). But he also examines the position of thinkers, like Murray, who hold that there are many absolute norms giving specific guidance for conduct in a variety of ways without ever conflicting with each other. Geisler, using the instance of Commander Bucher's capture by North Korea, argues that genuine conflicts can arise between absolutes (in the case of the illustration, the absolute to tell the truth and the absolute to protect the life of fellow humans). The attempt to eliminate conflicts among a large number of detailed absolutes results in a process of qualification that in effect nullifies the claim of the norm. He also rejects "absolute idealism," which simply acknowledges the necessity to violate one of the absolute norms and plead for forgiveness.

Geisler's alternative is "ethical hierarchialism," which sees some norms as more binding than others.

> [It] is so named because it maintains a hierarchial arrangement or ordering of ethical norms based on the relative scale of values they represent. It implies a pyramid of normative values which *in and of themselves* are objectively binding on men. But when any two or more of these values happen to conflict, a person is exempted from his otherwise binding obligation to a lower norm in view of the pre-emptory obligation of the higher norm.[32]

Obviously there must be a set of principles for dealing with circumstances in which there is a conflict between these objectively binding norms. Geisler has seven. 1) "persons are more valuable than things"; 2) "infinite person is more valuable than finite person(s)"; 3) "a complete person is more valuable than an incomplete person"; 4) "an actual person is of more value than a potential person"; 5) "potential persons are more valuable than actual things"; 6) "many persons are more valuable than few persons"; and 7) "personal acts which promote personhood are better than those which do not."[33] Knowledge of these principles can be intuitively grasped as well as known from biblical revelation. Moreover, the process of deciding between norms in cases of conflict can involve a kind of deliberation—but one that is duly concerned for the claim of the absolute norm. This scheme might be called a graded absolutism or even a contextual absolutism.

A modification of traditional absolutism is presented in yet another way in Millard J. Erikson's *Relativism in Contemporary Christian Ethics.* He proposes a normative casuistry that stands somewhere between the situationalism of Fletcher and legalism, but which is premised on a strong normative place for the will of God as a consistent and dependable indication of what is right. This view of God's will differs sharply from the view of God's will found in divine-command theories belonging to the relational motif. According to Erikson, "God has communicated rational, cognitive truth,"[34] and the Bible is to be read for a knowledge of the principles by which God has revealed his will. Some of these principles are specifically spelled out; others are stated in more general terms, but their objective character is paramount. They become the basis of a system which starts with the determination of the revelant principle or principles, moves to the formulation of rules or directives, refines such rules from general or generic to specific terms, and applies them to cases. "The law tells us what love really means by giving further delineations of it, thus showing various aspects of love. The law, as the embodiment of various principles of God's will and His nature, gives us a clearer indication of what the good and the right are."[35]

The use of the term law as traced in this chapter covers a wide range of ideas—from concepts that are practically identical with moral deliberation to a quite emphatic assertion that prescriptive specificity is a necessary aspect of a normative morality. The importance of law is stressed as a corrective to more permissive outlooks. An Anglican archbishop has heralded the role of law in maintaining liberty.[36] The Ten Commandments have become objects of written reflection by persons of very different orientations.[37] There is no doubt but that conceptions of law are enlarging and that there is a new appreciation of the value of rules for ordering human affairs. But this yearning for the specific delineation of the normative does not exhaust contemporary developments. A subdued situationalism and an enriched understanding or relational ingredients in morality continue to require the attention of the careful observer.

3

Variations of Relationalism and a Softening of Situationalism

When *A Survey of Christian Ethics* was written in 1964–65, thinking about ethical judgments in relational terms was a prevalent feature of much Continental Protestant thinking, and situation ethics were well known in England and the United States. Not only elaborate theological schemes mainly of interest to professionals, but popularized religious writings were emphasizing the contextual features of moral choice. Autonomous reasoning, moral philosophy, reliance upon natural law, code morality, casuistries in general, and moral theology as a normative enterprise were all under attack by such a large number of well-known voices as to spread the impression that Christian ethics was closely tied to the fortunes of a new morality—or at least to overcoming the disadvantages of an old one. The place of reason in moral judgments was accused of being dysfunctional in an ethic dependent upon the perception of and obedience of God's sovereign will. Specific descriptions of right and wrong were considered to endanger the spontaneous obedience characteristic of faith.

The influence of this set of ideas has been considerable, as is evident from the number of those persons whose thought has been discussed in the previous two chapters who have defined their approaches by making explicit contrasts to situationalism. Curiously, it has been situationalism and not relationalism which has been the prevalent foil. Situationalism may be a very easy target for criticism, since it is the most glaring and least richly furbished form of the relational motif. It tends to thrive on polemics and in turn become an object of counter polemics.

It would be misleading to suggest that the relational approaches have disappeared. A long exposition of a relational scheme will come first in the following account. Moreover, relationalism has influenced even those who did not adopt it fully. Many Roman Catholics have taken it into account and even in some instances accepted the terminology. Even those Protestants who have been pleading for greater attention to norms have often been at pains to indicate that they too are concerned about the particularities of cases and the necessity of taking circumstances into account. But the spread of influence is one thing; continuing development another.

Few Christian writers are more provocative than Jacques Ellul. One of his translators has said, ". . . if Ellul's work is to achieve its proper effect it should not be read as a definitive statement which one can appropriate only if assent is given but rather as a spur or stimulus which provokes new and exciting effort."[1] Even so, Ellul's continuing espousal of relationalism must be reckoned with. It was heralded many years ago in a book entitled *The Presence of the Kingdom*, which contains this passage:

> [A Christian ethic] . . . has nothing in common with what is generally called "morality," and still less with the Christian "virtues" in the traditional sense. It is evident that neither a theological decision, nor an intellectual argument, even if it be based upon the Christian revelation, will enable us to know the Christian ethic. At heart, this is a fight of faith: individual, and in the presence of God; and a living attitude, adopted according to the measure of faith of each person, and as the result of his or her faith. It is never a series of rules, or principles, or slogans,

and every Christian is really responsible for his works and for
his conscience. Thus we can never make a complete and valid
description of the ethical demands of God, any more than we
can reach its heart.[2]

Much of what Ellul has subsequently written has been consistent with that declaration. His works dealing with ethics are inter-
spersed with extensive writings about modern culture. Indeed,
much of Ellul's thinking about ethics spins off from his thinking
about the problems of modern society. Ellul's introduction to a
proposed systematic ethics was published in French in 1964 and
in English translation in 1969 with the title *To Will and To Do*.[3] He
has published the first of three projected subsequent volumes,
part of which was published in French in 1973 and the full
version of which appeared in translation in 1976 under the title
The Ethics of Freedom.[4] Still to come are *The Ethics of Holiness*
and *Ethics of Relationship*. The last of these may be even more
significant for the themes to which this chapter is devoted than
what is to be found in the volumes that have already appeared.

In his introduction to ethics Ellul presents a divine will theory
of ethics as categorical as that in any of the divine command
theories of his European forerunners. God alone is good, and his
will alone the source and measure of good. The divine requirements are always concrete rather than abstract, general, or inherent, and the effort to gain knowledge of good and evil independently of God is the great disobedience; ". . . the very act
by which man wants to decide what is good, wants to know the
good by himself, constitutes the sin."[5]

Because any search for a knowledge of the good unrelated to
God is sinful, and because there is no good that can be known
except in terms of God's will, and since in the Fall we have been
estranged from our relationship to God, only by accepting the
redemption in Jesus Christ can we establish a knowledge of the
good. "In scripture, there is no possible knowledge of the good
apart from a living and personal relationship with Jesus Christ."[6]
But while the good is defined solely by God's will and known
wholly in relationship to Jesus Christ, it is not capricious even if
it cannot have any content predefined in human terms. Only a

strange concept of God would lead us to conclude that defining the good as utterly dependent on God's will yields a capricious result. Interestingly, Ellul does sketch certain qualities as constituents of the good: "praying to God for others; interceding for one's enemies (Psalm 35:12–13); bringing about justice for men; defending the poor, the humble, the oppressed (Isaiah, Amos, Micah)."[7]

Ellul argues that no action, however trivial in consequence, can be morally indifferent, no question of procedure can be handled on purely technical grounds. Morality is a part—indeed a necessary and inevitable part—of life in the world, life under the conditions of the Fall. Because morality belongs to the Fall and is based upon certain errors—total disregard of the Christological basis of ethics, abandonment of a justificationalist approach, the substitution of philosophical construction for living dependence on God, and the attempt to postulate some essential nature to man—it results in a system of coercive necessity such as we experience living under political units like the state. This highlights the conflict between the nature of the good as defined by the will of God and the demands of morality as made in a secular society. While Ellul rejects all attempts to declare some aspects of creation good on the basis of natural law, nevertheless, he acknowledges that we cannot merely ignore or do without the morality which is part of fallen experience.

> This morality, strictly human, relative, temporary, and temporal, which is not the will of God no matter what form it takes, is nevertheless necessary. The Christian who is aware of its limits has absolutely no right on that account to treat it as false or useless. Morality is definitely not to be neglected, and as Christians we should persevere in taking it seriously. It is well to recall that Christian though we be we have not completely attained to the perfect stature of Jesus Christ and we are not yet in the kingdom of God. We are living on this earth at a given time in a given place. We are human beings like everyone else. By reason of that fact (and it must be thus, for Christianity is not a school for inhumanity) we share the errors and perceptions, the hopes and beliefs, the values and judgments, the virtues and limitations of the people of this time and place. It is

to be expected that, at the human level, we should judge to be good that which the people of this age call good. It is to be expected that we should feel judged when we disobey that good.[8]

Ellul describes the morality of this world—its diverse manifestations, the theoretical attempts at articulation and abstraction (confined in Ellul's judgment mainly to those societies influenced by the Judeo-Greek heritage), the problem of defining values, the social expression of moral phenomena, the role that variations of morality (moralism and immoralism) play in culture, and the transformation in the moral consciousness of the world occasioned by the rise of technology.

The concluding section of *To Will and To Do* opens with a chapter on the impossibility of a Christian ethic and ends with a chapter on the necessity of one. No Christian ethic can be constructed in the usual sense of that term—a definition of the good as a fixed knowable reality—since the biblical concept of the good as God's will prohibits putting another standard in its place. "The will of God remains perfectly free. It never becomes an abstract law of the presence of the one who puts it forth. It never becomes a philosophic or moral principle from which we would be free to draw conclusions, and which would remain as the origin of Christian reflection or conduct. There are no Christian principles."[9] Kierkegaard's insistence that obedience to the will of God can override even the normal demands of the ethical is valid. All casuistry is illegitimate because it is necessarily static and presupposes rules that need exceptions rather than a divine command that always comes so concretely as never to need interpretation. Moreover, the development of an ethic tempts us to posit our salvation in terms of conformity to norms rather than obedience to the will of God.

"And yet a Christian ethic is indispensable."[10] Such an ethic is a relative thing, as all morality is relative. Its major function is to prompt debate and dialogue about Christian responses to concrete questions.

Ethics is there as a sort of preparation. It does not have the right to furnish solutions for every problem, solutions which would be imposed with authority. It can only be the reminder that the specific conduct of the Christian is the indispensable consequence of his faith. It should at the same time be the equipping of the believer with an instrument of reflection and explanation concerning himself and his problems. Finally, it will be a reminder that the earnestness of the theological commitment should be registered in an earnestness of commitment in the world, and it will establish, for the particular time in which it is valid, the conditions and limits of that commitment.[11]

A Christian ethic understood in this way recalls God's actions across history; it gives us back the concerns of the world on a relativized basis; and it allows for the freedom in obedience that is at the heart of Christian discipleship.

These same themes, and particularly that of the freedom that we have in Christ to rise above the ethical, are restated in *The Ethics of Freedom*. In this book, as well as in *To Will and To Do*, Ellul writes with acknowledged indebtedness to Karl Barth. While the relationship with Christ logically seems to suggest that ethics is no longer necessary, experience suggests it cannot be so simply abandoned. For one thing, the church has too often been an opponent of freedom, and so it seems that nothing is more alien to freedom than theology and ecclesiastical organization. Then, too, the freedom in Christ is a freedom to stand alongside of that which is coming new into the world and to which creative adherence is good. Ellul shows, in an extensive discussion about alienation and necessity (both personal and social), that Christian ethics can begin only when we are provided with the ability to receive freedom. Christ exemplified freedom because he resisted the temptations (which would have made him, and left us, in bondage to economics, to power, and to spiritual pride). Ellul criticizes any ethic that attempts to capture God's changing will in a religious scheme or in an ethical law, either of which "binds man and effectively alienates him afresh."[12] In Jesus Christ we are made so free of the present social orders as to become strangers to them. In language representative of Ellul's transpositioning of usual meanings and also representative of ethics in the relational motif, he writes,

. . . obedience to God's will is itself freedom. Jesus exercises
the freedom of God himself when he obeys. We, too, are
invested with the freedom of God himself. It is thus by ful-
filling scripture as the will of God that Jesus bears witness to
his freedom in the temptation. For us as well being free men
means discerning this will in scripture and obeying it. [13]

Realizing that the term redemption has suffered a great eclipse
in contemporary theological usage, Ellul seeks to refurbish the
term (which he finds to be much stronger and richer in connota-
tion than the term liberation). Redemption denotes the fact that
much more is at stake in the ethical situation than a mere changing
of the external situation. Christian ethics involves having our
status changed from "being booked to die" (as are condemned
prisoners) to becoming "destined for life." Freedom flows from
the experience of being destined for life rather than for death, an
experience grounded in the fact that Jesus Christ has done a work
for all persons which overcomes the fate of alienation and creates
a new condition of being. While the work of Christ creates this
new condition for all, God does not force it on all persons but,
out of patient respect for the condition of creatures, "lets things
be." Only those who render service through a renewal of life as
made possible by this gift of freedom appropriate the reality of
Christian existence. Nor do all Christians attain their destiny.
Even so, the redemption present in Christ can overcome our
conforming and cultural bondage and set us beyond the natural
and even beyond the created order as experienced after the Fall
into the truth known alone in the saving work of Christ.

For Ellul, the very concept of autonomy (which many thinkers
find to symbolize freedom) is indeed a contradiction of the
understanding that "freedom is a situation made for us"—a situation in which we are placed rather than something which we
make by our wills. Freedom is thus, like justification, the equivalent of a gift. Not even sanctification can become the means to
merit it. Freedom releases us, therefore, not only from law but
also from alienation, and such total freedom is the precondition
of Christian responsibility.

One can achieve righteousness, humility, perseverance, and purity; one can engage in revolution and fight for the poor, but even all this is of little worth if it is outside freedom, i.e., if it is outside grace, outside generosity, outside the condition of life that Jesus came to set up for Christians. The works may be precisely those that are described in the Old Testament or Paul, but in spite of the external resemblance they add up only to secular morality if they are not done and lived out in freedom. They are then no more than an expression of kindly feelings which may approve of what Paul says and find it good and helpful.[14]

Freedom alone is what makes Christian ethics unique, "The importance of freedom as a condition of Christian ethics is so great that its presence or absence decides whether there is any Christian ethics or not."[15] The presence of freedom raises the Christian ethic above the level of morality—even above the kinds of moralism that turn freedom into anarchism or into other similar moralistic parodies of true freedom. Only the freedom stemming from Christ makes true choice possible (no free choice is possible for fallen humanity), and such true choice is a matter of immediate commitment, not of deliberation. "Righteousness has already been given to us. Our task is to choose it, to incarnate it, to live it out."[16]

Freedom releases us from bondage to law, from bondage to the world and its allurements, from our own created achievements, from the political powers, and even from the "flesh." Only when we thus break away from the several experiences and conditions of being in opposition to God, only when we achieve a "distance from ourselves" do we become free of the burden of the past. Then it is that we can respond to the future, not a future to be grasped or built by our efforts, but a future to be entered as a gift. Liberation in Christ frees us from bondage to the powers that subjugate persons—whether legally or religiously. It helps us to avoid making the commandment something binding apart from a relationship to God. Only after the law has become the expression of the liberator does it lose its constraining and binding quality of necessity and get placed in the service of freedom. But this freedom must be a source of service, not license, not the easy-going hypocrisy so prevalent in the contemporary Christian community.

> I would rather see Christians use phylacteries and keep the Sabbath in Jewish style than see them as they are, abusing grace and freedom, not even going beyond minimal demands, living as they like. This is the height of imposture. Puritans and literalists were far more serious than we who make a comedy of freedom, a pretext of grace, a mere emotion of faith, and the crassest social conformity of the Christian life. We are fornicators in relation to the love of God, appealing to our freedom to transgress his commandments a hundred times a day.[17]

The three-volume treatment of theological ethics by Helmut Thielicke has appeared only recently in English translation. Despite the size of these volumes they are somewhat condensed versions of the originals.[18] Thielicke says many of the things relationalists say—about the centrality of justification by faith, about the limitations of an imperative approach to ethics, about the importance of God's command to the believer, about the shortcomings of natural law, and about the impossibility of making ethical judgments in advance. But he also says things that differentiate him from relationalists like Barth and Ellul—about the importance of sanctification as well as justification, about the commandments as definitions of lawlessness which do give some guidance, about the necessity of coordinating the indicative and the imperative, and about Law and Gospel as constant partners. For Thielicke, "the Gospel without the accompanying antithesis of the Law turns forgiveness into a mere state of indifference."[19]

According to Thielicke, Reformation theology has failed to do justice to the extent to which the will of God is embodied through the orders of creation. Obedience to God's will is related to such orders, though not in a rigid or unequivocal way. Thielicke seeks an ethic of freedom that is distinct from legalism but also one that avoids caprice.

> The real chore in the matter of ethical decision is not that of performing the act itself, but that of searching and struggling

to discover what *is* right, what *ought* to be. Thus the norm which requires that I do my job honestly and well never arises in isolation, but always in conflict with other norms which set forth an equal claim, such as my duty to my family which also has a claim on me, or various other conflicting demands which the business world itself imposes.[20]

Although the analysis of conflict situations is important it can never produce a set of casuistical rules which can be applied with certainty. The demand of obedience is always uncertain, and therefore the Christian must decide in given instances what is, in fact, demanded by God's will. In doing this, advanced consideration of illustrative cases of conflict can provide clarification of the issues involved; but never certainty about what will be the right thing to do. Because Thielicke sees the law as making a claim he also sees forgiveness as overcoming objective guilt and examines compromise as a genuine and continuing problem for the Christian. (Thorough-going relationalism does not speak about compromise.)

The English translation of a long-published work by the Danish theologian Knud Løgstrup is now available. It extends the concept of relationalism to different parameters. The book begins with the declaration that "the one thing in our existence which the proclamation of Jesus touches upon more than any other is the individual's relation to the neighbor."[21] The key to our relation to the neighbor is the experience of trust, which we tend to take for granted until it is violated and we experience the pain of its absence. The ethical demand arises out of the need to protect this trust, to allow the other person to be what that other person is, neither neglecting that person's need nor overriding that person's autonomy. "The will to determine what is best for the other person—and to speak or remain silent, or to act in harmony with our insight into what we believe to be best for him—must be coupled with a willingness to let him remain sovereign in his own world."[22]

The ethical demand is radical because it requires us to come to the neighbor whether or not it is a pleasure to do so. Although the other person has no right to make the demand, nor we to impose it in any way that violates individuality, the very functioning of political process depends upon sharing. Law, morality, and conventions protect us from each other, yet may also create closed approaches, especially if the psychic impact of such norms has been altered without corresponding modifications of their functional consequences.

The radical demand, since internal, is invisible, but it is refracted through experience in a variety of ways. The demand, by virtue of its radical dimension, sets no limits, that is, is "silent" about specifics.

> It is characteristic of everything that Jesus said—so far as it has been transmitted to us—of every story and parable, of every one of his answers in conversation or argument, of every concisely formulated utterance, that it is a proclamation of the demand which in itself is silent. This is the intangible in his proclamation, that which foredooms all efforts to systematize it. Jesus' proclamation contains no directions, no rules, no moralizing, no casuistry. It contains nothing which relieves us of responsibility by solving in advance the conflicts into which the demand places us. [23]

According to Løgstrup, any attempt to spell out the requirements, i.e. to create a "Christian" ethic, would become ideological and would permit the kind of self-deception that breeds fanatical devotion to causes or oversimplifies the statement of obligation. Therefore, the demand will stand over and against all efforts, unilateral or mutual as the case may be, to control existence. The acceptance of life as a gift enhances the capacity to trust, as does also the experience of forgiveness.

A modified divine command theory of ethics has been advanced by Robert Merrihew Adams. Unlike the types of divine command theory that rule out all valuing independent of God, Adams argues that we must evaluate in order to know that certain kinds of commands or actions are logically impossible or inconceivable in relation to the kind of God in whom we trust. According to Adams, ". . . it is not essential to a divine command theory of ethical wrongness to maintain that all valuing, or all value concepts, or even all moral concepts, depend on beliefs about God's commands. What is essential to such a theory is to maintain that when a believer says something is (ethically) *wrong*, at least part of what he means is that the action in question is contrary to God's will or commands."[24] Judeo-Christian ethics has many conceptual ingredients of a superhuman, non-naturally objective, law that do come into play in deciding that a particular course of action simply cannot be a version of a divine command. But to say that these concepts have priority over all human laws does not require that their priority must also be asserted over every law, over every normative judgment.

Facing the charge that such a modified divine law theory plays havoc with the theological demand that God be the object of highest allegiance, Adams holds that it is unrealistic to expect obedience to God to effect a sharp and total overthrow of normal valuations.

> In analyzing ethical motivation in general, as well as Judeo-Christian ethical motivation in particular, it is probably a mistake to suppose that there is (or can be expected to be) one only thing that is valued supremely and for its own sake, with nothing else being valued independently of it. The motivation for a person's ethical orientation in life is normally much more complex than that, and involves a plurality of emotional and volitional attitudes of different sorts which are at least partly independent of each other. At any rate, I think the modified divine command theorist is bound to say that that is true of his ethical motivation.[25]

Adams notes that Barth scorned the idea that God's *power* over us is the reason we should obey. Barth, by holding that it is God's grace that is the locus of his claims upon us, is saying in effect that it is the quality of God in which the believer reposes trust. The ascription of moral qualities to God is a normal and legitimate aspect of Christian theology. ". . . the believer normally thinks he has at least a general idea of what qualities of character are in fact virtuous and vicious (approved and disapproved by God). Having such an idea, he can apply the word 'good' descriptively to God, meaning that (with some exceptions, as I have noted) God has the qualities which the believer regards as virtues, such as faithfulness and kindness."[26]

Relationalism has been set forth not only in divine command versions but with the category of responsibility. H. Richard Niebuhr's articulation of this category has been widely influential since its appearance in 1963. This influence appears less in whole systems emulating Niebuhr's than in a wide ranging utilization of the idea in a number of different approaches. It would be impossible to trace that influence in detail, but some representative examples will suffice to demonstrate how widely the idea has permeated the field of Christian ethics.

In their discussion of the role of the Bible in ethics, Bruce C. Birch and Larry D. Rasmussen have this to say about deriving norms from the biblical materials:

> Whatever the particular method, it would need to be in keeping with Christian ethics as at root relational or response ethics. The touchstone for Israel's morality and that of the early church is always the faith-experience of God. All the elements used in determining which behavior is most fitting in a given set of circumstances take their form and function from this faith relationship. This means, to cite but one example, that rules, principles and other norms in the decision making process are viewed as expressive of underlying relationships, indicating their kind, quality, and content. The rules, principles and other norms take their authority from the defining relationships, not the reverse.[27]

Discussing the several aspects of the moral self and how it comes to decisions, James B. Nelson holds that the relational approach is valuable and that H. Richard Niebuhr's use of it helped to "raise precisely the kinds of issues that Christian ethics must now press into further conversation with the social sciences."[28] (A treatment of Nelson's view of moral agency appears in Chapter 8.)

Perhaps the most surprising appropriation of the relational framework appears in Roman Catholic moral theology, where it has been used as a means of turning away from the ahistorical approaches to natural law contained in the manuals. Charles Curran has worked out a defense of this model with reference to other efforts to accomplish the same transition. He considers that the attempt of J. M. Aubert to go back to the original frameworks of Thomas makes far more place for changing understandings of the human situation than are present in later theorists. He reports an effort, even on the part of one of the defenders of natural law, to put greater empirical inquiry into its use. He considers, among other newer efforts, the attempt of John Giles Milhaven to develop a Christian morality in consequentialist terms. In Curran's view this is too much influenced by the assumption that we control our worlds. Curran himself opts for a relational-responsibility model which he deems superior because it can combine "both empirical data and the creative and transcendent aspects of human existence."[29] Elaborating upon his disagreement with Milhaven, Curran notes,

> Milhaven originally was concentrating primarily on the question of absolute norms in moral theology and denies such norms on the basis of his appeal to the ultimate importance of consequences in determining our actions in these cases. The perspective I have outlined considers rather a very basic posture for our total moral life and thus does not want to reduce our total ethical posture to the model of consequences or of man-the-maker. On particular questions involving the existence of absolute norms, I too would agree on the need to evaluate and weigh all the elements involved in the light of my relational vision of human existence. A relational understanding of reality incorporates the historical and changing aspects while denying any eternal, static hierarchy of relational values. Obviously in particular situations one determines what is good in terms of what will promote his understanding of relational values.[30]

The third version of the relational approach has gone by the name situation ethics (sometimes called the new morality). It may have attracted the greatest attention, and was the object of considerable discussion.[31] Clarion calls on behalf of situationalism as such have become increasingly rare. Even a book which identifies with the situational approach and makes the case for its compatibility with biblical understanding has this disclaimer in its preface. "The reader . . . will find in these pages none of the sensationalism that characterizes so many treatments of this subject."[32] Another writer, sympathetically assessing the significance of the situational approach for Christian ethics, nevertheless takes pains to suggest that the significance of the approach and its ties to tradition had been easily obscured when it was presented too enthusiastically as some utterly new thing.[33] James Gustafson once called the attempt to polarize ethics according to the situational model "A Misplaced Debate." Perhaps it has almost come to be a dying one. In its stead has arisen a more complex and thorough-going effort to understand the interplay of norm and context in Christian ethics.[34]

II

Implementation

4

Ongoing Forms of Institutionalism

Belief in the contributions made by structures of justice and order to the implementation of Christian ethical decisions has been extended and to some extent enriched since 1965. This has not been an auspicious period, particularly in the United States, for affirming the importance of institutionalized arrangements for achieving social objectives. However, belief in the importance of institutions has not evaporated from the scene and its continued appearance is an essential part of the continuing story.

We examine first Helmut Thielicke's discussion of the political order in the second volume of his *Theological Ethics*. He takes note of the changes that have occurred in the forms and functions of the state since Luther developed the two-kingdoms version of Augustinianism. Thielicke examines the shift from authoritarian to democratic means of controlling political affairs and concludes that this shift does not require us to abandon the Pauline/Lutheran formulation since "all the theological teachings associated with it can be transferred without difficulty to other kinds of state. Theirs is simply one of a variety of forms which the state has taken and may take."[1]

But although the shift toward the democratic state does not require us to abandon the Pauline/Lutheran framework, the rise of the totalitarian state in which politics and economics become spheres unto themselves—a condition to which Thielicke applies the term autonomy—creates problems for the traditional formulation. When the businessman, for instance, comes to feel that economics are governed only by considerations of the market and its pressures, he retreats into a private religious inwardness that Luther would have considered alien. When the political leader concludes that political affairs are governed only by power, as Bismarck did, that leader tends to separate politics from Christian morality. Under such circumstances the orders become normless, ambivalent, and potentially demonic.

It is no small wonder then, Thielicke argues, that modern ideological tyrannies abandon the felt tension between the orders as representative of creation and the orders as examples of fallen normlessness, and turn politics into the practice of sheer rivalry for domination. Under such conditions it is no wonder that "conscience as the retention of an unconditional awareness of norms is a power-consuming luxury which one cannot afford within the bestiality of a history ruled by the laws of the jungle."[2] Christian theology bears the heavy burden of counteracting this conclusion—a task it can perform by reconceptualizing an institutional understanding of the state.

The state "is ordained by God as a necessary remedy for corrupt nature . . . [but the state] contains an element both of judgment and of grace. It involves judgment to the degree that, in its restraint of evil, it calls fallen man in question. It is an order of grace to the degree that God's gracious preservation is in many ways displayed in it."[3] This formulation of the role of the state prevents us from equating the state with creation, setting it above moral scrutiny. It also helps to prevent the making of a false antithesis between views that subordinate the state to the individual and those that subordinate the individual to the state. That antithesis can be overcome only when both the individual and the state are related to God's reality.

Asking whether the state is a legal society (in the sense it exercises only power) or a moral society (in the sense that it must justify the exercise of power by appeals to principles and values), Thielicke examines how law and morality both coalesce and differ. If a legal system is based only on power, tyranny results. A viable state must be grounded in an ethical understanding of the purpose of human creation, though ethical obligation may sometimes require actions that go beyond legal requirements and may also require resistance to the state. A large subsequent section of Thielicke's work deals with the borderline problems of revolution and opposition to individualized requirements of the state.

Power, which is an aspect of politics, is ambiguous; "power as such is neither good nor evil, no more divine or demonic than the sex drive or technology."[4] But power must be subject to scrutiny and control, which can be accomplished by stressing the role of authority in sovereignty in contrast to the mere exercise of force. Power is exercised with authority when it elicits autonomous response from subjects rather than mere submission. An office has authority when the person who exercises the office "stands under the same binding norm as those who are subject to him." Authority also involves the personal qualities of the officeholder. It must be built up through a long period of love and loyalty. (In saying this Thielicke differs significantly from many institutionalists who differentiate sharply between the power of the office and the personal qualities and attributes of the officeholder.)

A second way of keeping power in check is structural, and involves institutional safeguards in the form of the distribution of power. Although the state must be sovereign, its power must be spread in such a way that it cannot be monopolized in a single place.

> . . . the distribution of powers is necessary because fallen man is not able to handle uncontrolled, monopolized power. Such power becomes an instrument of egoistic expansion and thus poses a threat to the freedom of others. By guarding against the misuse of power, the distribution of powers thus has the positive task of safeguarding freedom, of making freedom possible in the political sphere where a variety of power constructs necessarily arise.[5]

The distribution of power to which Thielicke refers should involve both the division of decision-making within government and the division of duties between the government and private agencies. The protection of human rights depends to a significant degree on the institutional self-limitation of government. "In other words, of all the tasks involved in the distribution of powers the most important is that the machinery of state leave some of its powers to the responsibility and initiative of free citizens and of relatively free institutions, i.e., those which have large powers of self-direction."[6]

In *Ethics and the Urban Ethos* by Max L. Stackhouse we find an institutional understanding of social ethics developed with reference to the modern setting of human life as dominated by the artifacts of technology. Stackhouse modifies and extends the traditional views of *civitas*, covenant, and commonwealth by relating them to the modern city as the product of technical reason. The city becomes a setting in which the crucial dynamic of modern society takes place: ". . . whether intellectuals like it or not, modern man lives in the city, and in the urban ethos it produced, the epitome of all man-created social order with its distinctive forms of existence."[7]

The city is a constructed artifact, but should not be envisioned merely as a locus of concentrated population. It is a place having particular qualities of existence—an ethos. Consisting of "the subtle web of values, meanings, purposes, expectations, obligations and legitimations that constitutes the operating norms of a culture in relationship to a social entity,"[8] this ethos is as evident in a military-industrial complex (many functional parts of which are located in rural settings) as it is in skyscrapers and apartment houses.[9] The complexities involved in the city are enormous:

> [The city] allows greater specialization of function and increased participation in voluntary activities. It requires effective rationalization and bureaucratization of routine activities, but allows more direct participation in certain mass political activities that have large-scale and long-term significance. Urban civilization involves complex organization and increased interdependence which some see as extending the range of human responsibility, and others see as adding undue forms of im-

personal stress. Patterns of community identity become diffuse under the impact of urbanization, a phenomenon which some see as providing freedom and mobility, while others see as bringing anonymity and rootlessness. Relationships tend to become pragmatic or functional, which some interpret as demystifying and liberating and which others see as mechanizing and dehumanizing.[10]

It is important to bring the city under some rational direction, moral cohesion, and conceptual integrity. These require an institutionalizing process, since ". . . society inevitably implies some conception of controls for the sake of human fulfillment through rules, management, authority, institutionalized structures and roles."[11] While such controls cannot be imposed by religious orthodoxies or ecclesiastical courts, secular equivalents are standing ready to oblige. Ethical concern must deal with the city in terms of structural relationships (macro-ethics), not merely in terms of personal relationships or private life-styles (micro-ethics). Such ethical concern must focus on systemic issues and criticize those structural maladies that "prevent the possibility of maturity and love, that deny manhood, womanhood, and the viability of maturity and love to whole groups."[12] Stackhouse is particularly critical of "the notion that liberation involves overthrow of structured, institutional life," which he feels "does not take account of the historic tendency of man to spontaneously devour his neighbor when there is pure spontaneity."[13]

Stackhouse addresses the problem of power in the urban ethos. In contrast to political theories that make "political punch" the main explanation of what happens in the urban ethos, he contends that power is an outcome of cultural and institutional relationships between systemic entities. These entities can be understood according to different models. One model, that of the power-elite, is inaccurate because it assumes that a few people on the top are manipulating things. Another model, in many respects the obverse of the first, holds that power has become so diffuse that it is hard to get anything accomplished. This is also unsatisfactory. Stackhouse believes that the relationships that shape the policies governing institutional and cultural relationships depend upon "value sets" that inhere in both leadership functions and institutional arrangements. Thus, if we want to analyze how the urban situation functions we should "ask what norms are built into the various institutions that select leadership, define priorities, influence the judgments of those in positions of responsibility and power."[14] In doing this we must look, not only at the typical "orders" but at voluntary associations that adopt particular value-sets for particular circumstances.

Much of Stackhouse's argument is given to the relationship between social theory and "credo." A credo is a "purposive, explicit, critical conceptual apparatus of interacting specified norms."[15] It is not merely an ethical construct abstractly derived from normative considerations alone, but must be "confirmable or disconfirmable according to its relationship to technical data about the structures, projections, and functions of human life and institutions in a given ethos."[16] Because they are related to experience, credos are provisional and subject to revision.

One of the important ingredients in a viable urban ethos, which must take into account where a society is headed, or ought to be headed, is the biblical vision of *shalom*.

> It involves quite concrete elements of basic security, equitable responsibility for, equitable access to, and equitable distribution of economic, political, and cultural resources. It involves a polity based on a law that is written on the hearts of men, and a sense of vocation pervading the community.[17]

Shalom cannot be grasped with programmatical certainty. As an eschatological vision it guides and inspires rather than provides a "right" agenda that contends against all alternatives by aiming to shut them out. Programmatical certainty comes from both the right and from the left, in both reactionary and revolutionary forms. Both are dangerous, although "the absoluteness of a moral claim by the oppressed is superior to the absoluteness of the claims of the oppressor, as both Jesus and Marx recognized. But moral ambivalence still exists because both, and not just the oppressor, falsely identify the concept of liberation and new creative order exclusively with their own community."[18]

It is impossible to have the fulfillment envisioned eschatologically without relating the personal and communal aspects of experience to one another. Revolutions tend to seek social fulfillments without paying adequate attention to personal dimensions; privatized religious movements tend to pay attention to personal fulfillments without paying attention to social dimensions. Stackhouse would balance these: "those who see human institutions and patterned necessities as part of the realm of grace as much as spontaneous spirituality of imagination and image will acknowledge the capacity for institutionalization as one of the marks of an authentic spirit."[19]

Stackhouse employs theological and ecclesiological terminology in examining various social options. For instance, he uses the Christian doctrine of the Trinity as a model for social construction—the Father stands for the creative and just order, the Son for transformed personal identity, and the Spirit for the freedom of the righteous. Rather than turning to secularization as the clue for cultural adulthood, Stackhouse boldly presents ecclesiology as a model for understanding the future. ". . . no vision of the future, and no doctrine, crucial as they are, can sustain themselves or constitute a complete *credo*. They cannot survive without a structured constituency."[20] Stackhouse amplifies the church/sect framework proposed by Weber and Troeltsch to suggest patterns of organization that arise in the urban center and conform to neither type. Noting the uniqueness of the denomination (which fits neither church nor sect pattern exactly), he proposes three ways of looking at social structures that are analogous respectively to the Catholic, the Calvinist, and the Sectarian models. The necessary ingredients for the future include institutionalized patterns of order, opportunities to have personal identity in the midst of ordered structures and community participation, and participation in an ongoing thrust for justice and righteousness. Each of these ingredients has institutional features.

> Law, pattern, organization, convention are not *necessarily* oppressive false forms that need to be dispensed with, nor are they eternally fixed, especially when understood as involving nurture, sustained and loving support. Instead they are potential

structures that are more or less appropriate to sustaining human projects. It is true that these can become systematized oppression and violence when patriarchally structured or when divorced from the vision of the Kingdom; but then the difficulty is not to dispense with all signs of order, but rather to establish those patterns that do perform the critical functions that lead to creative patterns.[21]

Stackhouse presents a complex understanding of institutionalism. In the final chapter of the book, he analyzes the function of law and suggests that the control of law is a function of credo and legitimation rather than of clout. In any showdown with violence, credo is more determinative in giving shape to law and adjudicating disagreements. Ultimately, credo depends upon a sense of the sacred in the broad meaning of that concept; ". . . the future does not demand secularization so much as it does a sacredness through a necessary theological reinterpretation of an urban *credo* and its ethical implications."[22]

James Luther Adams has made significant contributions to thinking about society in institutional terms and has inspired many to explore the issues of religion and society in scholarly depth. He has been a rare individual who has contributed greatly to Christian social thought without publishing a book devoted wholly to a systematic development of his own position. He has published many articles and given many lectures. Additional clues to his thinking are provided in the work of his former students and his friends, who hold him in highest esteem and have often learned as much from his letters and bibliographical counsel as from his writings.

Adams's thought breaks with the two-kingdoms tradition of mainstream Protestantism and flows from a careful reassessment of the left-wing heritage. But it emerges as an expression of institutionalism, and is referred to as such both by himself and by his interpreters.[23] Voluntary associations mediate between the individual and the larger collective orders such as the state. They perform prophetic functions because they are independent of coercive structures, and they exercise a kind of power that is rooted in God's law and God's love as a source of creativity. They are means for "the institutionalizing of gradual revolution."[24] They help to preserve pluralism in society; they presuppose the right of association and thus "they protect the freedom to criticize, the freedom to express newly felt needs, the freedom to define the situation in a new way, and the freedom to instigate or to implement social change."[25] Voluntary associations work for change, but by persuasion and demonstration rather than clout. They presuppose law but keep up the pressure for the redress of grievances and the attainment of justice.

In an essay prepared in 1979, Adams relates the concept of voluntary associations to the concept of "mediating structures" then being given currency by Peter L. Berger and Richard L. Neuhaus. These mediating structures exist between the individual and the state and, when functioning as they should, provide a political and ideological dynamic which keeps the control of the state from becoming unilaterally dominant. By participating "in these spaces that function as wedges preventing overweening powers from presenting a united front against criticism," the citizen helps to develop a source of social power that is complex in its dynamics but crucial in keeping the process of institutionalization from becoming an end in itself, and from making unqualified demands for total subservience. All through the Hebrew-Christian experience—in the qualification of kingship by covenant, in the independent status of the religious prophets, in the defiance of the demonic rulers by early Christians, in conciliarism as a challenge to papal centralism, in the dispersion of power by congregational polity, and in the federalism advocated by Madison—the idea of separated powers has served well to enhance freedom while nevertheless recognizing the importance of corporate action.

The intimate and ultimate—indeed, all parts of the interrelated world—the individual, the middle structures, the government, the society, and the divine creative ground of meaning are held together by covenant. The bonding and binding quality of covenant, the ordering principle, is promises. God is the promise-making, promise-keeping reality upon which we ultimately depend as the reliable, creative, sustaining, judging, community-forming and community-transforming power . . . This power is manifest not only in interpersonal relations; it can appear also in institutional behavior, even if only ambiguously and incompletely. The separation of power in society makes possible intervention in the name of the promises, intended to prevent bondage to any finite power.[26]

Carl F. H. Henry approaches the task of Christian social ethics from an evangelical conviction that "the church's primary duty is to expound the revealed Gospel and the divine principles of social duty, and to constrain individual Christians to fulfill their evangelistic and civic responsibilities."[27] He considers it very crucial whether we deal with the problem of social justice—which surely must be dealt with—by having the institutional church act in a political way or by urging individual Christians to fulfill civic duties in a proper and conscientious fashion. He feels that action by individual Christians is preferable to political action by the church, but stresses the importance of the teaching function of the church and the home, in which respect for law is cultivated and where belief in the value and meaning of work is instilled.

Henry argues that Protestant forces in America have neglected "the method of *evangelism* and the dynamic of supernatural *regeneration* and *sanctification*. Instead, they have resorted to a series of alternative forces—at first, moral propaganda and education, then legislation, and more recently, non-violent public demonstrations and even mob pressures against existing laws."[28] Of four strategies he identifies for effecting social change (revolution, reform, revaluation, and regeneration) he is very critical of a revolutionary strategy that advocates violent or compulsive overthrow of constituted social institution. In contrast, he favors regeneration, which he contends is the classic Christian position. This seeks to renew the socio-historical condition rather than to destroy it. The options in between—reform and revaluation—are both revisionist rather than revolutionary, but they would be more useful if they were not rendered questionable in the current situation by too close and frequent association with humanistic and secular assumptions. Henry is crystal clear in his objection to any form of social change (particularly as accomplished by violence or pressure tactics) that is not instigated from and accompanied with the regeneration of minds and hearts. In contrast,

> Supernatural regeneration . . . is the peculiar mainspring for the social metamorphosis latent in the Christian movement. Man's spiritual renewal vitalizes his awareness of God and neighbor, vivifies his senses of morality and duty, fuses the law of love to sanctified compassion, and so registers the ethical impact of biblical religion upon society. Man's personal dispositions are thus enlarged for sacrificial service, and his benevolent desires are qualified by a new moral power. The familiar evangelical call to be "born again," the high task of winning other men to Christ, the pervasive work of the Holy Spirit in sanctification, all contribute to the basic motivations of social impact. Under such divine constraint the believer impresses his influence on society through the family, in immediate neighbor relations, in daily work pursued as a divine vocation, and, as a citizen of two worlds, in fulfillment of civic duties.[29]

The concluding sentence of the foregoing paragraph evidences a deep commitment to institutional means of expressing the consequences of regeneration. Changed outlooks and attitudes result in utilization of established orders—not in a process of struggle for a new social system. This orientation is evident in the subsequent discussion in which Henry details how work can be transformed from its present frustrating and oppressive drudgery by coming to view it as a source of service to God rather than by changing its conditions and format.

> The real drudgery of today's worker results not alone from his machine-bound existence on the assembly routine, but from a distaste for work itself. Because of his secularized misunderstanding, he dissociates the daily task from all mission either for God or man. Even the corporation executive complains that he is an "organization man," a mere cog in the wheel of business activity.[30]

While the worker on the assembly line seemingly has to change attitudes rather than circumstances, Christian employers can, in so far as they "refuse to conform their organizations to the established, sometimes corrupt, patterns of the secular economic world . . . have an opportunity to shape higher and exemplary types of employer-employee relationships and activities."[31]

Turning to the factors that govern the Christian stake in legislation, Henry acknowledges that Christians can live, as indeed they have done and still do, under quite different forms of political order. He believes that the problem of preserving a significant role for religion in politics is presently complicated by the fact that both in totalitarian situations (where the problem is obvious) and in democratic societies (where secularization makes the problem just as real though less noticeable) the political order pursues its agendas without reference to the will of God. While the church should be concerned with the revealed will of God for the political order it should not "force its distinctive requirements upon society as a whole through techniques of pressure and compulsion."[32] It is not the function of government to achieve a social Utopia, or to embody the Kingdom of God. Thus the church should not try to achieve a Christian society by political action and it only creates difficulties when it attempts to do so.

The devout person is to respect the positive law of the state in all matters and not merely in those particulars that seem to accord with the Decalogue or at those times when the state is upholding Christian religious principles.

> The Christian's duty to support the State includes observance of tax laws and laws of community order such as speed limits, parking regulations, and so on. He is not to begrudge such obedience to statute law, as if the demands of civil government represent an unavoidable encroachment upon Christian liberty. The Christian community must promote public morality by personal example and a positive spirit toward the State. This requirement is implicit in various scriptural injunctions."[33]

The responsibilities of the church toward the state include the duty to make clear the proper role of civil government in the divine ordering of human relationships. While it is to counsel obedience, it is also called to make clear that the state is not to be idolatrized, to declare that the function of the state is valid only as an instrument through which citizens work for the common good and not as an instrument of domination. The Christian will resist totalitarian claims that arise when the state transgresses the proper limits of its function, and will also resist the ethical relativism that abounds in our times and erodes the efforts to hold the state in check. The Christian will be clear that the state is obligated to do justice and to respect the rights of individuals.

The laws of the state, which must serve justice, are to apply to all persons equally. They prevent persons from injuring one another. The function of law is enhanced by the sound practice of the profession of law when exercised as a Christian vocation. The freedom to proclaim the Gospel is essential to the health of the state, and political activity by individual Christians is a proper "pre-evangelistic" duty. "Every search for Christian perspective on political and social matters must identify righteousness as the New Testament's central interest, in contrast to modern motifs such as security and even freedom."[34]

Henry calls all Christians to some form of political responsibility—a responsibility to be exercised by every citizen and not merely those who hold office. "In respect to giving time and talent to the State," he writes, "the Christian's chief duty as a citizen of the community is that of civil obedience."[35] Obedient to the civil order, the Christian will seek to create a truly informed public opinion, to create an atmosphere in which the rulers will, and can, seek to reform social evils, and will engender new levels of personal self-discipline and moral earnestness as foundations of a sound social order.

Henry's thinking about these matters has been further developed in another book, entitled *A Plea for Evangelical Demonstration*. In this book, no less than in his first book on social ethics, he calls evangelical Christians, whom he accuses of long neglecting social witness, to a biblically oriented role in society. This involves stressing justice as a corollary of redemption. Henry criticizes revolutionary efforts to overthrow existing orders, and he finds the agendas of the Social Gospel, of neo-orthodoxy, and of the revolutionary advocates (all of which arose to fill the vacuum left by the default of evangelicals) to be respectively too pacifistic, too subjective, and too Marxist to provide an adequate social program. Addressing issues raised by theologies of revolution, Henry acknowledges the necessity of using power in the public realm alongside of the use of love in personal relationships —but such power must be employed under institutional safeguards.

> . . . the fact is that Scripture points to civil government as the responsible tool for justice, and not to the radical secular alternative of coercive revolution. According to the New Testament, civil government is God's stipulated instrument for preserving social justice and public order in fallen human history. Although political authority is capable of abuse and being abused, it is divinely responsible for social justice and order, and supplies the most ideal framework for their public preservation in this fallen world.[36]

Like any Calvinist, Henry acknowledges the possibility that a corrupt government may need to be replaced. "It is clear that Christian conscience cannot support a government that is deemed to be wholly corrupt, and that in such circumstances revolution becomes an unavoidable option." But in the very next sentence he blunts the force of this by remarking, "But can any government except an antichrist state be catalogued as totally corrupt?"[37]

Henry argues that we must stimulate respect for the righteous will of God, and that unless we bring the status quo under "searching, searing, divine scrutiny" we will get conditions that require revolutionary action. He contends that it is just as wrong to do nothing about social wrongs as it is to treat them with premature and abortive civil disobedience and revolution. Instead, we must witness to the regenerative power of God to alter social institutions by working through regenerated individuals.

The period of the late 1960s and 1970s has seen discontent, not only with the institutions of society in general, but with the institutional church itself. The cultured despisers of ecclesiastical institutions are nothing new, but when professed Christian theologians pronounce the institutional church moribund and abandon hope for its reform or renewal in institutional forms, the issue is joined on a different level. The book by Charles Davis, *A Question of Conscience*, was a particularly strong indictment of ecclesiastical structures,[38] but there were many versions of religionless Christianity that seriously questioned the importance, even the validity, of institutional expressions of Christian fidelity.

This account of institutionalism in recent Christian ethics would not be complete without mention of those whose voices (or, pens to be more exact) were raised in defense of institutional Christianity. Vatican II, although greatly changing features of the church, nevertheless produced important documents that examined institutional possibilities and have inspired subsequent reflection.[39] Among Protestants, James Gustafson argued that "as long as there is a religious faith that is shared by a group of people, there will be institutionalization of religion."[40] While Gustafson recognized the changes that take place in institutional life, either by default or by purposive direction, he argued that the church, no less than any other corporate body, must decide upon its purposes and "have the institutional authority and the means to achieve these purposes in the society and the historical period in which it lives; institutional power is a requisite for its existence."[41]

Thomas C. Oden also argued for the importance of the institutional church. In doing so, he presented a rationale for institutions that in one way or another would be representative of all those whose thinking has been referred to in this chapter.

> Far from being inescapably dehumanizing (as they are often conceived), institutional structures are the necessary matrix of the humanizing process. Far from being inevitably stultifying to human freedom, institutional processes are the necessary milieu out of which human freedom springs and develops. The well-conceived institutional structure may be celebrated by the

Christian community as joyfully as the individual freedom that thrives within it.

Institutional structures are programming devices to free us as individuals from the endless, frustrating process of trial-and-error experimentation in the construction of human environments. They enable us to bank on the funded resources of human social experience.[42]

5

Politics in Operational Terms

This chapter considers a political rather than an institutional model for thinking about the exercise of Christian responsibility in society. *Political* as it is used in this chapter means the exercise of power and influence in operational terms. There are many gradations of opinion between institutional and operational ways of thinking about society, but the differences between the central expressions of one motif and the central expressions of the other are clear and undeniable.

Representative of a growing group of evangelical scholars who are convinced that privatized individualism in religion is unbiblical, Richard B. Mouw believes that the Bible addresses our corporate lives with political images and categories. His approach differs sharply from that of Carl F. H. Henry, although both are interested in promoting greater social concern among evangelicals. In *Politics and the Biblical Drama*, Mouw identifies with Gustavo Gutierrez's call for a political theology which does its work as a "critical reflection on historical praxis."[1] He shows that many human relationships, such as the family structures, which are often considered to be quite unpolitical, are increasingly understood in political terms as it comes to be recognized that power and authority operate in them as well as in larger and more impersonal structures of society.

Mouw's analysis of the nature of politics is organized around four stages of the biblical drama: Creation, the Fall, Redemption, and the Future Age. Mouw holds that politics was present in the Creation before the Fall. This means that it will be a part of redeemed human existence and not merely an aspect of a sinful world which will be eliminated by God's saving work. Politics can be an instrument of cooperation as well as coercion, part of God's intended design for the final order and not merely a "left-handed" restraint upon sin, present only during the interim between the Fall and the Final Consummation.

This position rules out believing, as did Hobbes, that political structures are an alien imposition on human nature. It presupposes the importance of both individual and social relationships. Finally, it underscores the fact that relationships of individuals to each other and to larger social units can be used either creatively or destructively.

The original creation included a politics marked by equality between human beings, but subordination of one human being to another arose because of the Fall. Sin affects politics by introducing the impulse to manage and control others rather than to trust and respect them. But sin can manifest itself not only in the process of engaging in manipulation and oppression but also in acquiescing to them. Sin causes the institutional and political machinery intended to enhance human freedom and social interchange to be corrupted into a self-serving instrument of domination. Even Christianity itself has been a source of domineering manipulation. But just as this does not invalidate Christian faith or Christian community, so the corruptions possible in politics do not require its repudiation. Marxists, who look toward the systematic "de-politicizing" of human relationships, are misled in believing that the state will wither away. They contradict their own premises when they affirm the continued necessity of administrative procedures to maintain human life. Since politics is part of the original creation, it is to be practiced and redeemed rather than shunned or abolished.

Mouw considers the life of the church to be a portent of redemption and of the contours of a redeemed society. According to the Belgic Confession of 1566, the church is the place where the word is preached, the sacraments administered, and standards of discipline maintained. It is, therefore, at one and the same time a listening, a sacramental, and a growing community. To carry on these roles the church needs not merely institutional features that turn inward but organic features that turn outward.

> The marks of the true church also have analogies to important elements in the external mission of the Christian community in the world. First, while the people of God, viewed from the perspective of their internal life, must form a listening community, they must also function as a proclaiming people in the larger society. The message they have received is not to be hidden from the world. The people who have heard the good news must also bear the message to others. Second, the people who have been served by Jesus Christ must in turn become servants in the world he came to save. Third, as those who have been—or are in the process of being—disciplined by God's word, they must become discipliners in the world. These three requirements, which we have drawn as analogies to the institutional functions of preaching, sacraments, and discipline, correspond closely to the biblical "offices" of prophet, priest, and king.[2]

In order to exercise its functions in the contemporary world, the church must obey the biblical call which is "to identify with the oppressed, especially with the economically oppressed."[3] Mouw affirms this, yet warns of the difficulties involved and repudiates simplistic suggestions that too easily suppose that the elimination of one or another social order will overcome all the problems of history. Concern for the poor is a fundamental test of fidelity to the biblical tradition, but that concern must not be motivated by, or take the form of, coercion or manipulation of others. Renewal of the internal life of the church and efforts to bring that life into conformity with the Gospel must go with the exercise of external influence.

Mouw considers the political sphere in terms of Saint Paul's categories of the principalities and powers. The powers have to do "with various forces, spheres, and patterns of our lives which present themselves to us as possible objects of idolatry."[4] While they can serve to help order human life, when they are given ultimate instead of proximate importance "the Powers become despotic lords over us. Those spheres of activities and corresponding reference points which were originally intended as means of harmony and partnership now serve as forces of alienation, and lead us finally to ultimate disintegration."[5]

Reviewing the disagreements among biblical theologians as to whether the work of Christ intended to free us from the continuing rule of the powers or actually to undercut their functions, Mouw contends "that Christ has exposed the Powers and penetrated their territory."[6] Mouw compares the thought of Hedrikus Berkhof, in which the possibility of Christianizing the powers is suggested, with that of John Howard Yoder, in which the strategy of "revoluntionary subordination" is advocated.[7] Mouw opts for the Reformed contention that "it is proper to attempt to bring contemporary societies (in addition, that is, to the contemporary church) into some degree of conformity to theocratic standards."[8] Political processes and structures are necessary, they are subject to discriminating judgments between just and unjust expressions, and the search for the righteous society includes active interference in the civic affairs of both covenantal and pagan communities. While Mouw acknowledges the dangers and temptations, he concludes that Christians can be legitimately involved in politics, including the occasional, critically appraised use of violent forms of coercion.

In a final chapter on eschatology, the political nature of dispensational "Israel-monism" (found in those fundamentalists who look for Christ's return to a Davidic throne in the nation of Israel) is contrasted with the views of those who consider the United States to represent the wicked city of Babylon as depicted in Revelation.[9] The one has no hope for any nation except Israel; the other has no hope for any nation. In contrast, Mouw considers it is at least possible

. . . that political institutions as we now know them—along
with various other structures and activities associated with the
culture-building life of a people—will not be destroyed in the
last day, but will be purified and transformed into fitting
dimensions of the kingdom of God. If this is the proper way to
view matters, it is not enough to say, as we observe the
institutions and practices of our political/cultural life, "Created,
but *fallen*." We must also say, "Fallen, but *created*."[10]

One of the fullest, most complex, and intriguing discussions of
politics written within the period covered by this survey is Paul
Lehmann's book *The Transfiguration of Politics*. Lehmann argues
that obedience to the Gospel in our time requires that "Christians
must abandon their time-honored addiction to legitimacy;
whereas revolutionaries could find in the gospel perspective and
power for the fulfillment of their promises and the liberation from
their fate."[11] Casting doubts upon the legitimacy of both institutional conservativism and revolutionary agendas, Lehmann seeks
"to show *that the pertinence of Jesus Christ to an age of revolution is the
power of his presence to shape the passion for humanization that
generates revolution, and thus to preserve revolution from its own
undoing. All revolutions aspire to give human shape to the freedom
that being and staying human takes; and all revolutions end by devouring their own children.*"[12] The transfiguration of politics possible through the Christian faith enables this cycle to be broken
and room to be made for what is human in man and in society.

Revolution, according to Lehmann, is intimately connected
with the passion for humanization. It is the manifestation of
impatience with hypocrisy and failure in existing orders—an
impatience that reaches toward the freedom symbolized in the
identification of Jesus with the messianic tradition of Israel's
prophets. "The Christ story is the story of the presence and
power of Jesus of Nazareth in and over the ambiguity of power
in human affairs. It tells in word and deed of the liberating limits
and the renewing possibilities within which revolutionary promises and passions make room for the freedom to be and stay
human in the world."[13]

In the chapter "Jesus, Marx and the Establishment: The Power of Weakness and the Weakness of Power" Lehmann shows why the state cannot serve as the instrument of revolutionary promise. In Marxist governments it fails to attain the freedom that is supposed to follow revolution, and in the democratic societies of the West its bureaucracy defaults on the achievements of justice that are intended. The presence of Jesus Christ transforms the options between submission to and rebellion against existing authorities (as these are practiced in conservative and revolutionary politics respectively) into *"a much more subtle practice of the love of neighbor that recognizes in existing authorities the great divide between a self-justifying legitimacy that ends in the tyranny of order and a self-justifying rebellion that ends in the tyranny of anarchy."*[14]

Submission to existing authorities understood in this way does not mean acceptance of the status quo, but a temporary surrender that avoids the misdirections that result when revolutionary thrusts become as much their own self-justifying agendas as the conservative establishments they seek to overthrow. While the revolutionary impulse is "nearer to the center and direction of God's purposes for human life in and for the world"[15] than the defense of the status quo, only insofar as the revolutionary surrenders fanaticism to reconciliation will an unjust situation be transformed. Likewise, for existing authorities, becoming aware of the presence of God's truth means accepting the judgment that the time has come when they shall be the Establishment no longer.

Using a thematic exegesis of the story of the transfiguration, according to which things that are changed by the ingression of things that are not, the argument observes that Jesus rejected withdrawal from politics (as represented in the monasticism of the Qumran community), as well as the attempt to force history to a programmatic conclusion through a battle with the existing order (as favored by the Zealots). In rejecting both, Jesus still firmly sought a new humanity even though doing so led to violent upheaval. In this he was in a sense closer to the Zealots than to the members of the Qumran community but identified with neither. More than one hundred pages in the middle of Lehmann's book are devoted to an analysis of three contemporary revolutionary movements in which Lehmann sees signs of transfiguration.

These considerations lead Lehmann to espouse a biblical politics based upon: 1) "an incarnational hermeneutics [that] seeks to discern the word and will of God in, with, and under the discernment of the times in which we live";[16] 2) a correspondence between the biblical and human meaning of politics that weds piety and politics; and 3) the transfiguration of revolutions when they are saved from devouring their own children.

> The pertinence of Jesus Christ to the question of revolution is that he stands at the juncture of revolutionary freedom and fate. His presence in the human story transforms revolutions from harbingers of futility, violence, and death into signs of transfiguration in the power of a saving story. The Christian or messianic story documents its "saving reality and power" in a paradigmatic movement from a politics of confrontation to a politics of transfiguration whose code words are: *submission, silence*, and *transfiguration* itself. These code words identify the boundaries toward which and within which the dynamics of revolutionary passion, promise, and struggle are liberated from self-destruction and shaped instead for a new and divinely appointed order of human affairs in which time and space are ordered so as to make room for freedom.[17]

Lehmann calls for an embrace of revolutions that relates to them, not only under them in support, but over them in potential distance, even criticism. Only through such critical distance can revolutions be freely embraced and not become new ways of destroying the human. Revolutions reverse the order of political priorities by making freedom the foundation of order and making justice the foundation and criticism of law.

Resistance to the pursuit of justice as founded on freedom and humanity frequently takes violent forms in a fallen world, revealing the moral bankruptcy of politics as rooted in the defense of established systems, values, and orders. Violence is not a moral factor to be either rejected or embraced on the basis of ethical judgments, but an eschatological happening to be accepted as and when the pursuit of freedom elicits a violent response from a fallen order. Revolutionary thrusts must resist reduction to a single programmatic policy, since such a policy may become in turn a new order of self-justifying repression. Revolutions may risk but not deliberately embrace violence, for if they embrace violence programmatically they may be their own undoing.

The transfiguration of revolutions, i.e. the process of saving them from their own undoing, involves: 1) keeping central the thrust toward liberation so that questions of tactics (as debated between "hard" and "soft" revolutionaries) do not make commitments to a strategy more crucial than the goal; 2) keeping central an element of transcendence, so that thought about humanization is not (as in utopianism) falsely believed to rise above the arena of political reality; 3) the preservation of the realization that no presently identifiable or specific action ever totally grasps or embodies the humanization at the heart of God's will for man; and 4) overcoming the idolatry which absolutizes commitment to cause—be it the preservation of the established order or the pursuit of its overthrow.

The book ends by suggesting analogies and similarities between its view of social process and Kuhn's understanding of the process of change in scientific paradigms.

The rise of interest in social questions among evangelical Christians is anything but a unified expression of a single point of view. Not only are there momentous differences about particular issues and questions, but there are also theoretical differences about how Christian social responsibility is to be exercised. Some evangelicals are strong defenders of institutionally constituted order. Others, who will be discussed in the next chapter, are intentional perfectionists who advocate various kinds of withdrawal from both institutionalized orders and from the exercise of operational power. Still others assert the centrality of power in the shaping of policy and urge their Christian associates to become politically active in its use.

Paul B. Henry, for example, chides evangelicals for their failure to take the phenomenon of power seriously. His admonitions read like those of the Christian realists whose thinking about politics prevailed in the 1950s.[18] Henry argues that changing hearts is not enough because questions have to be faced and matters of moment dealt with under circumstances in which hearts are not changed and only the coercive power of the state will insure necessary consequences.

> In the nineteenth century, Karl von Clausewitz defined war as "politics by other means." For the very essence of politics is the use of power—the power to determine who in a given society gets what, how, when, and where. The political system is nothing less (although hopefully something more) than the institutionalized means a society employs to resolve questions incapable of being resolved voluntarily without the use of the sword. When Jimmy Carter spoke of a government "which is as loving as its people," he should have been reminded that government acts not as an agent of love, but as a final resort to force when love, compassion, and voluntarism have failed.[19]

Politics, as understood by Paul B. Henry, allocates resources and values. The allocation of resources benefits some and deprives others of possessions and privileges; the allocation of values determines the decisions which steer policies toward one goal rather than another. Politics is not necessarily the brutal scramble for self-interest, though it cannot be realistically understood without taking into account the tendency of individuals and groups to maximize their self-interest at the expense of others. "Politics thus operates amid the conflicts of self-interest and the conflicts within individuals and groups relative to private interest versus public interest."[20] One of the important avenues for Christian witness is, therefore, to be vocal about the moral implications involved in the decisions that shape public policy.

Politics inevitably involves "the use of the sword to establish compliance with the allocative decisions being made in the name of the state."[21] Arguing against those who would rely on voluntarism to overcome the evil of society, Paul B. Henry admits that a change of people's hearts may affect the value systems shaping political choices, but that would not by itself solve the total political question.

. . . to repudiate involvement in affairs of state in the name of Christian love implicates us in sins of omission for not having done what we might have done to affect public policies for the good. I shall concede that involvement in affairs of state implicates us in sins of commission, and that the policies of state fall short of absolute justice and the demands of Christian love. But to avoid involvement in the struggle for justice under the power of the state is to bear responsibility for the unspoken word, the unfulfilled deed, and the withdrawal from the decision-making process which removes Christian witness from the political struggle. And how can one claim fidelity to the norms of love and righteousness at the top of the moral ladder if he is unwilling to serve also the norm of political justice with all of its relativities at the lower rung of the moral ladder?[22]

In the case of Paul B. Henry, as in the case of the Christian realists whose thought is so similar, the political agenda is a liberal one. The essays that are associated with Henry's, though not necessarily sharing his operationalism, likewise share a generally liberal outlook on particular matters. With the rise of political action in groups like the Moral Majority, this coincidence between political realism and social liberalism has changed, and as of this writing all the theoretical and social consequences are yet to emerge. It is, however, already clear that urging Christians to become politically active does not ensure that particular kinds of policy will be advanced.

The books by Mouw and Lehmann, and to a lesser extent the view of politics advanced by Paul Henry, can be described as theologies of politics. They examined the nature, functioning, and legitimation of politics in light of the Gospel. We now turn our attention to a movement calling itself "political theology," which arose in Europe and has been mainly but not entirely confined there. Three figures are usually identified with political theology: Johann Metz, the Catholic author of *Theology of the World*; Jürgen Moltmann, author of *Theology of Hope*; and Dorothee Soelle, author of *Political Theology*.[23] All three start with an analysis of the contemporary world as a secularized pluralistic ethos in which the presence of God is acutely absent and in which an anthropological perspective is the necessary starting point for theology.

These authors call for a different way of thinking theologically, one that repudiates the personalistic response of existential theology and overcomes the separation of Christianity from the social dimensions. Metz argues that *"the deprivatizing of theology is the primary critical task of political theology."*[24] Dorothee Soelle says, "The question . . . for any theology is whether it makes men more capable of love, whether it encourages or obstructs the liberation of the individual and the community."[25] She finds the historical-critical method to have been insightful in freeing us from dogmatic theology's attention to fixed truths that are asserted without regard for the relativity of historical experience, but she decries the prevalent tendency to couch the results of the method in existential terms that are largely personalistic and insufficiently aware of the socio-political setting that shapes them. The agenda we must pursue is to extend the method of historical-critical thinking to include the analysis of our own present social experience and its consequences for our way of understanding things.

> The historical-critical method is not threatened from without by an alleged "new wave" of scientific and historical hostility, but only by its own characteristic inconsistency, specifically in a three-fold manner: first, because it limits itself and does not include present day ecclesiastical and social structures and their ideological superstructures; second, because it overlooks the historical mediation of the contents of Christianity; and finally, because it exempts [from its analysis] apparently invariable and always valid structures of faith and their appropriation. As long as historical criticism remains true to the Enlightenment spirit in which it is grounded, which means asking critically about historical mediations and conditions, and as long as it preserves the essential features of any historical methods (which according to Troeltsch are criticism, analogy, and correlation) then not only does it have nothing to fear from a sociopolitical theology that is consciously committed to the same methodological principles, but on the contrary political theology car-

ries on in the best tradition of liberal theology and preserves precisely the achievements of criticism, analogy, and correlation, while enriching them with refinements from sociology and sociology of knowledge.[26]

Theological formulations are integrally related to political experiences. Any inference that theological formulations can be separated from their social settings (as dialectical and existential approaches to theology suggest to be the case) seems to Soelle to be an ideological illusion. Political theology holds that "only what is appropriated and mediated politically, only what is relevant to the life of everyone in society, can be regarded as understanding."[27]

Noting appreciatively Bultmann's enterprise of demythologizing, which reformulated theological constructs in light of the perceptions of modern science, Soelle argues that it is now necessary to make another conceptual revolution in which the political conditions of present existence are taken into account with the same urgency with which Bultmann took scientific thinking into account. The ". . . ideological criticism [of contemporary society] takes the place of demythologization for us."[28] Looking at the significance of Jesus for faith and action, Soelle suggests that we must assess the benefits that Christ has furnished, not merely seek to imitate him or follow patterns he followed.

> It is not a matter of compiling in a biblicistic sense materials pertaining to the political activity of Jesus and using them to establish whether or not he was a revolutionary. The main thing is not to describe his concrete behavior and imitate it, but rather to discern the intention or tendency of that behavior and to realize anew his goals in our world. Thus is it meaningless to ask: Was Jesus a revolutionary? Where did he stand on violence, on landed property? Instead, we as his friends who affirm the intention of his decision must attempt for our part to declare where we stand today on revolution, property, or violence.[29]

We find the importance of critical method as an ingredient in political theology further explored in a collection of essays, *Religion and Political Society*,[30] among the contributors to which are Jürgen Moltmann and Johann Metz. The essays in this collection argue against any totalistic or absolutizing unity, whether ideological or bureaucratic in nature, that obscures the diversity in human affairs or points toward a utopian vision that forces all present action to serve a single objective. Moltmann's essay argues that theology must recognize its inevitably political nature, which precludes a neutral stance, but must also resist any identification with a political program (whether in the form of a totalitarian agenda or the consensus of civic religion in a democracy). In short, theology must be political in order to render prophetic criticism over every extant political system. The task of criticizing national religions or civic religions (which appeal precisely because they unify populations and provide nations with self-justifying myths) involves identifying with the victims of oppression. Institutions cannot exercise genuine social criticism of themselves because they are wedded to social respectibility and the mores of the dominant society.

Johann Metz's chapter entitled "Prophetic Authority" opens as follows:

> Any theology that intends to be critically responsible for the Christian faith and its transmission cannot ignore "social" and "practical" issues. Furthermore, genuine theological reflection does not permit itself to be isolated from the problems of the public good, the law, the present status of freedom, etc. Moreover, theology must recognize a fact that has become especially clear since the Enlightenment and the post-Idealist critique of religion: namely, the Church is indeed always active as a political power, even before it adopts any explicit political position, and thus prior to any debate about the basis of this or that actual political attitude. For this reason theology considers the Church's assumption of its own neutrality as either naive or deceptive. Through the development of a *practical-critical* hermeneutic, theology seeks to prevent the Church from identifying itself uncritically with particular political ideologies. Accordingly, theology strives to prevent the Church from degenerating into a purely political religion, or at least from functioning as such. Understood in this way reflection on the political horizon in theology would be a form of *practical-critical* ecclesiology.[31]

For Metz, the critical problem is church authority. The ways in which the church and theology have understood authority in the past are incompatible with Enlightenment understandings of freedom. This incompatibility is evidenced, not only in the counter-reformation of the Roman Catholic Church (which has openly resisted the thrust toward freedom in the Enlightenment) but in Protestantism as well (which has uncritically allowed itself to be assimilated into a bourgeois version of freedom). The church must develop an authority that witnesses to freedom rather than against it. In so doing it will draw upon the *memoria* of Jesus Christ who sets us free from sin repeatedly. "The recollection of Jesus Christ is a courageous and liberating remembrance that breaks through the limitations of a one-dimensional understanding of emancipation with its progressive destruction of real freedom. Through its challenge, the *memoria* of Jesus Christ forces us constantly to change ourselves if we do not want to lose it in the long run."[32]

Metz does not deny the place of institutions; he simply subordinates it to functional measures of effective authority. In developing the new kind of authority we must call into question the paternalistic framework of traditional ecclesiastical practices, we must be willing to embrace the "strangeness" of our historical world, and we must be willing to undergo new experiences rather than to withdraw into a new sectarianism. "The Church must understand and confirm her existence in the midst of our so-called progressive society as the witness to and bearer of a dangerous memory of freedom."[33] In doing this, she takes her cues from Jesus Christ, not so as to sharpen her separation from the world, but so as to break "through the structures of the dominant consciousness of our age, a one-dimensional way of looking at things which hides the fact of oppression and injustice from us."[34] The eschatological element preserves us from identifying any existing achievement with the final one, and thus ensures the continual vitality of the prophetic stance.

Many of those who take this stance would see their commitment as what John Vincent describes as "acted parable" or a "prophetic sign." This concept derives from the biblical tradition of symbolic actions, as in the prophets and Jesus. The acted parable achieves symbolically by a small significant action that which is needed by the whole society. The acted parable thus also exposes the actions of mainline society by proposing and exemplifying a radical alternative. The radical alternative is at least intended to be politically responsible. It can function as a "unilateral initiative," an experiment whereby a new solution or policy can be tried out by committed persons in one place, so as to be an experimental model for the whole society.[35]

Political theology arose in Europe. Many of its themes— particularly the need to overcome oppression and the emphasis on praxis—are central in the liberation theologies that have developed in other places in the world. The possible significance of political theology for Great Britain has been explored[36] and the term has also been applied to agendas in both of the Americas.[37] Liberation theology, into which political theology easily moves, is a larger trend and is even more explicit in reconceptualizing the theological task. It will be treated separately in Chapter XI as a new framework for approaching ethics.

A widely mentioned criticism of political theology appears in Edward Norman's *Christianity and World Order*.[38] Norman decries the attempt to define Christian faith in political terms and the role of the clergy as agents of social change. He disapproves the use of secular ideals of tolerance, flexibility, and compassion to indicate Christian virtues. Many of Norman's criticisms are aimed at specific developments in the life of church bodies like the World Council of Churches. He objects to the efforts of third world delegates to shape the agenda of the Council around a Marxist critique of contemporary capitalist society and to the increasing tendency to define the importance of faith in this world's terms rather than as a concern for the destiny of the soul in an everlasting life. Norman's critique shows how political one becomes even in arguing that the church should not be concerned with politics.[39]

Norman's arguments about the nature and appropriate functions of the church remind us that the church itself is a possible object of attention and scrutiny. At the end of the last chapter we discussed the attention focused on the church as an institution.

The church may also be viewed as an arena of political activity. Keith Bridston points out that the church is more honest and healthy when it understands the political aspects of its own corporate life than when it denies them in an effort to think of itself as holy or sacred. While not denying the organizational features of the church (polity), he argues that it is equally important to consider the operational dynamics (the politics) of ecclesiastical bodies. Identifying with political realism and applying it to the life of churches, Bridston examines them in functional terms that openly acknowledge the power factors at play within their operations. He indicates that serious distortions and misunderstandings occur when ecclesiastical disputes are otherwise imagined. With respect to disputes that arise in churches, he observes,

> . . . [the church-related] dispute becomes scandalous not because of the heat but because of the humility! That is, the rising temperatures are generated by the power dynamics operating. But the heat becomes oppressive when it has inadequate outlets. Thus again, it is not the fact of power but the denial of power that is politically destructive. The public does not understand the dispute. They impose on their church leaders a style of "humility" which does not allow them to be honest about the power dilemma they are facing, or candid about all the factors, "personal" or otherwise, which are generating the political heat.[40]

Just as secular politics provides for the acknowledgment of power, so church politics would be healthier if the sacred/ceremonial roles of office could be separated from policy-making roles. We should not, therefore, decry the efforts to politicize the churches by making them democratic and subject to the will of the membership. "Only those religious institutions, causes, and movements which foster rather than inhibit this participatory democratic spirit have any prospect for survival in a post-magical world."[41] Just as the British have maintained a healthy democracy by separating symbolic offices from policy offices, and the bureaucratic civil servant from the political policy-maker, so the church will be healthiest if political processes are allowed to take place openly and without the limitations that inhere in having to maintain ceremonial integrity or bureaucratic objectivity. Church politics can become a high calling that can be "not only an art and a science but also a spiritual vocation."[42]

The close collaboration with the world involved in both institutional and operational patterns, and particularly the willingness to use power for the achievement of social consequences, leaves many uneasy. They distrust the implied acquiescence in violence that is entailed, and they believe it is possible to implement Christian purposes more intentionally. Their way of thinking is the focus of the next chapter.

6

The Rejection of Accommodation and Intentional Alternatives

Not all Christian ethicists find the embrace of institutions or involvement in political struggle to be acceptable ways of implementing Christian responsibility. A number, from quite different backgrounds, radically challenge the accommodation to principalities and powers that began when Constantine recognized the church and Augustine worked out the theory of the two cities. These thinkers are critical of the ambiguity of institutions and of the fruitless or demonic character of the violence upon which politics depends. Some of them are critical and reject accommodation without offering alternatives; others have more confidence in Christian patterns of special dedication.

The writings of Jacques Ellul are emphatic concerning the fallen nature of institutions and the fruitlessness of power for serving Christian purposes. One of the images that Ellul uses to develop his ideas is the image of the city. He does not use the term in the sense that Augustine did; rather he has in mind the contemporary urban structure that concentrates population in a small geographical area. Ellul has no doubt but that the city is built by those who are estranged from God—those who are rebellious and even guilty of murder. But despite this fact, we cannot escape to the country. There is no alternative to which we can turn to avoid the guilt involved in building and living in the city. Just as Israel was forced to live captive in a geopolitical structure—"really obliged to follow the politics of the world"— so "this adventure has been reproduced at every turn of God's work because it is impossible to completely refuse the world's work and be immune to the spiritual bearing of that work."[1] Or, to put it even more forthrightly:

> Standing before a city, man finds himself faced with such a perfect seduction that he literally no longer knows himself, he accepts himself as emasculated, stripped of both flesh and spirit. And acting so, he considers himself to be perfectly reasonable, because the city's seduction is in fact rational, and one really must obey the orders of reason.[2]

The city stands under the judgment of God. It is under the curse. This means Christians cannot look to the city for the solving of problems. Yet God has not forbidden Christians to live in the city. Rather, we must live in it, and without first transforming it. "For man is not responsible for making the city something other than it is."[3] The city is the "hub" of the state, and all that is true of the city is also true of the state. Neither can be reformed—remade so as to be free of their rebellion and contradiction. Moreover, God does not ask us to seek another place. Rather, ". . . our job is to lead the life of the other inhabitants of the city."[4] We are to accept involvement with the city and all its shortcomings, because forgiveness comes along with judgment, because the command to leave the city does not come until after the city is destroyed, because the city (like the state) is "occasionally an instrument of God" in history. Ellul knows that this view is not easy to accept, that it scandalizes us. "What outright injustice on the part of God thus to use an instrument, then condemn it in his wrath, while the instrument has only done his will. But to reason in this way is disastrously to oversimplify, to betray a mind unwilling to bow to revelation."[5]

Even Jerusalem, the holy city, carries the curse. "[She is] built in blood, and living in sacrifices, crime, and war."[6] Nevertheless,

Jerusalem is a sign of hope, a place that makes God known, a place in which he abides. Jesus also condemns the city; he uttered woes against the cities of his day. At places Ellul is categorical: "Jesus speaks only to [the city] to curse her."[7] At other places he leaves the door ajar for some hope, if not for the city, at least for those who live in it.

> A two-dimensional being cannot imagine three-dimensional space, and we cannot ourselves imagine four-dimensional space. We can calculate what it would be, but we cannot live it. Thus the city can calculate, but not live any word concerning God's order. But the miracle, the restoration of God's order in her midst, . . . can be received and lived. . . .
>
> Jesus' very words show that the city could have understood, could have grasped the sign. She could also have recognized herself as beaten, as included in a truly new order of things.[8]

The strategy of withdrawal is ruled out by Ellul just as much as belief that the city will be reconstructed in harmony with God's intention. "We are the city, and this is one of the most important facts of our generation. It is absolutely indispensable that we realize what that means for us, for our actual life."[9] The city lives by the exercise of power in military terms, which is a contradiction of the Gospel; the city lives as a parasite—sucking up strength and sustenance from those who produce the things that sustain life (though the city does produce intellectual ideas); the city attracts people to its confines and then subjects those people to regimentation under conditions of filth and degradation. Yet, cities will continue to form, to grow, and to come through historical changes. And, at the end of history, the last fulfillment will unfold according to the image of the city—the new Jerusalem— and not in a pattern of an agrarian paradise. The tensions in Ellul between the sense of doom under which he holds that the city lives and the sense that we can relate to the vitalities of life only through that same city makes Augustine's description of the ambiguity attached to living in the earthly city seem moderate in comparison. Perhaps this is so only because Ellul's writing has the forcefulness which is possible with the use of a more contemporary idiom; perhaps Ellul comes very close to breaking the dialectic and urging outright rejection.

Ellul is critical of politics in ways very similar to the ways in which he is critical of the city. He decries the trends in recent European (and by inference American) history that have increased a tendency to turn to the state for the solution of social problems. The state, in his judgment, is not amenable to control by the people, nor are the organizations of power. Neither can solve problems; they merely facilitate a tolerably equitable amelioration of difficulties. Politics, like the city, is a realm of sin and blind alleys.

Most of what Ellul writes about politics is negative and condemns its thirst for control over us, its divorce from morality, its perversion of liberty into conformist submission, its dependence upon warping truth and controlling propaganda. Yet, just as the sinfulness of the city does not legitimize movement to a "country," neither does the sinfulness of politics justify the taking of an apolitical stance: ". . . to become apolitical is to make a political choice, and as a result apoliticism hides some very definite political choices. The idea that one can escape politics by being nonpolitical is just as absurd as the political illusion itself."[10]

Two faint suggestions seem to modify this rejectionistic stance. One holds that "man may eventually participate in politics, but on the condition that he knows exactly what he is doing."[11] Having a critical distance that knows how limited and illusory the prospects of political achievement are alleviates the situation somewhat. So does the creation of associations that are "totally independent of the state, yet capable of opposing it; able to reject its pressure as well as its controls, and even its gifts."[12] Such associations grow out of the struggle against the official political order and have some usefulness in qualifying its hegemony. These associations have some institutional qualities. Even so, there is no redemptive significance either to the institutional form of the city or to the operational realities of politics.

In Ellul's discussion of violence we find a similar pattern, although Ellul is not so much concerned to question the role of the citizen as to condemn participation in violence. His strictures against traditional justifications for the Christian use of the sword include objection to the compromise between church and state occasioned by Constantine's recognition of the church and criticism of the casuistic legitimation of Christian involvement in the use of force (although Ellul concedes that the church in the middle ages did, by using force, protect the weak and maintain peace among the powers). Ellul also refutes the arguments he ascribes to contemporary political and liberation theology that violence may be a Christian duty.

Ellul holds that it is impossible to control violence or ensure that it will serve the cause of order, justice, or peace. Consequently he opposes just war theory as well as any other means of trying to hold violence in moral check. He believes violence is wrong, is against the teachings of Jesus and the witness of the early church, and has been wrongfully and tragically utilized in Christian history. Addressing arguments supporting the contemporary use of violence on behalf of the poor, Ellul asserts that it is a serious miscast of Christian understanding to hold that "man-come-of-age does not need to practice humility and resignation; [that] he can and must affirm his domination."[13] Ellul professes to be aware of the claims and frustrations of the poor and the oppressed. He understands the conditions that prompt resort to violence and even understands why the oppressed take to it.[14] But he does not think Christians are to join in violent crusades for justice or that the violence of the disinherited will free them. "To be on the side of the oppressed and at the same time to have to tell them that their explosions of violence are futile and will bring no real change—this is the most thankless position anyone can take."[15]

In his treatment of violence Ellul asserts its totalistic, endemic, continuous, uncontrollable nature. Violence simply cannot be checked, he argues. In comparing violence to institutions he makes this very revealing observation.

> Here is an important point: On the level of institutions or values, it is impossible to distinguish between ends and means. On this level only, the traditional distinction holds up. Institutions exist only for and through men. But while institutions are always the creation of human beings, and whether they are just

or unjust, effectual or ineffectual depends entirely on the people who use them. Values have no meaning except as they are lived by man! . . . But violence always breaks and corrupts the relation of men to each other.[16]

William Stringfellow, like Ellul, is a lawyer and lay theologian. He also, like Ellul, has had a past history of active involvement in social action. He has developed an increasingly critical assessment of institutional life, particularly of American institutional life. He has concluded that American life and culture have currently become so antithetical to the biblical vision of God's intentions for historical and social existence that Christians must now live as "aliens" in a strange land. Stringfellow is deeply critical of the failure of politics to serve love and justice. He condemns "the failure of moral theology, in the American context, to confront the principalities—the institutions, systems, ideologies, and other political and social powers—as militant, aggressive, and immensely influential creatures in this world as it is."[17] He calls for an ethic of social renewal that takes account of the realities and becomes aware of how they thwart much of what the Christian Gospel calls for in the way of human interaction.

According to Stringfellow, the Fall is crucial for understanding the contemporary political situation—and it is an understanding of the contemporary situation with which Christian ethics must work. The Fall is central to understanding the current position and actions of the American nation. America has become a new Babylon—guilty in our time and circumstances of the same apostasies and atrocities as was the city known as Babylon in the imagery of the book of the Revelation of John.

Central to Stringfellow's thesis is the contention that "biblical faith . . . possesses an essentially empirical orientation,"[18] which means that it judges the realities of a particular and existing order rather than search for an idealized conception of a perfected society. He accuses Platonism, Marxism, and Buddhism of projecting an idealistic or mythological idea which is either extra-, pseudo-, or post-historical in locating the social enterprise. "In relation to the world as it is, in the everyday existence and activity of principalities, nations, and human beings, each [of these views] establishes similar arbitrary and artificial polarities between lofty concepts and realpolitik, between what ought to be and what is, between vision or thesis or dream and actuality."[19]

Two cities, Babylon and Jerusalem, become the images or symbols through which a biblically informed faith wrestles with the particular empirical realities about which Christians must be concerned. Babylon symbolizes the negative, demonic, and destructive; Jerusalem, the positive alternative. Just how negative Stringfellow believes Babylon to be comes out vividly in his own rhetoric: "This Babylon is allegorical of the condition of death reigning in each and every nation or similar principality. The fallenness of this same Babylon is empirically evident and, indeed, enacted everywhere, every day, in the experience of specific nations."[20] Stringfellow is not arguing that some nations under some conditions become Babylons while other nations under other conditions become Jerusalems. Rather all nations as they are empirically found in a fallen world are indeed Babylons—and the task of the Christian is so to live as not to be a citizen of them.

> . . . biblically speaking, the singular straightforward issue of ethics—and the elementary topic of politics—*is how to live humanely during the Fall*. Any viable ethic—which is to say, any ethics worthy of human attention and practice, any ethics which manifest and verify hope—is both individual and social. It must deal with human decision and action in relation to the other creatures, notably the principalities and powers in the very midst of the conflict, distortion, alienation, disorientation, chaos, decadence of the Fall.[21]

The positive ground from which this way of deciding and acting can be carried out is as a citizen of Jerusalem, which, in contrast to the fallenness, doom, and death of Babylon, stands for holiness, redemption, and life. This Jerusalem is found in Christ's church.

Stringfellow repudiates the institutional way of looking at the relationship of church and state. Institutions can claim to be legitimate only insofar as they stand up to measures that are taken solely from the Bible. This means that the Church does not acknowledge the claims of any political principality simply because it is lawfully established, but only when it does the will of God. Even the idea that governments are lawful when they derive their authority from the consent of the governed, which has figured so largely in thinking about the legitimacy of democratic governments, while provisionally plausible as a test of legitimacy, has to bow before a yet higher standard. Only the relationship that existed before the Constantinian recognition of the church can provide the ground for judging the nation. The Constantinian arrangement placed the church under worldly political authority and thus acculturated and corrupted the church. Stringfellow notes that to reverse the Constantinian arrangement would call for much more than a revolutionary overthrow of one order postulated on such an arrangement to another order similarly postulated. "On this point, theologically, there is very little distinction to be made between those who long to reestablish an old status quo and so indulge nostalgic sentiments, and those who aspire for a new status quo and so become revolutionary idealists or ideologues."[22]

According to Stringfellow, institutions are simply not subject to a moral control compatible with the Gospel. Hence, no useful purpose is served by the Constantinian arrangement. Because of this and because the second advent of Christ means the destruction of the ruling powers and principalities of this age, the whole approach which seeks legitimacy in the political order must be abandoned.

> It is the critical relationship of the expectation of the judgment, held in a sense of imminence by the biblical community, to fallen political authority that prompts me to search for another way of dealing with issues of conscience and obedience than that traditionally furnished by the rubrics of legitimacy or order. My rejection of these customary criteria is, I reiterate, not so much out of a conclusion that they are false as that they are biblically inappropriate and, in some of their versions, misleading. They fail to take sufficiently into account the stories of creation and fall, they minimize or sometimes ignore the vocational issue as it emerges from these stories, they are too abstract, too arbitrary, too artificial, too narrow, they

have become far too conditioned by the Constantinian environment and too convenient to its comity favoring the status
quo.[23]

The issues raised by Stringfellow are enormous in scope and
radical in depth. They call for a reconstruction of a life-style and
witness within a radically reconceived church that resists current
regimes and every other post-Constantinian set of institutional
identities. The saints who follow this strategy are not so much
being disobedient to civil law as denying the legitimacy of that
law. They simply refuse to follow the world's standards and thus
will be considered foolish by the world; they refuse to utilize the
political wisdom of a fallen world and thus will suffer defeat as
judged by that worldly wisdom; but they will know justification
as a gift of God's word.

John Howard Yoder's book, *The Politics of Jesus,* has become
as frequently cited in discussions of social ethics as Paul Ramsey's
Deeds and Rules in the discussion of norm and context. Yoder's
book is pivotal because it develops a position that rejects the
Augustinian foundation upon which both institutionalism and
operationalism depend while also challenging the individualistic
and apolitical withdrawal of his own Mennonite heritage as well
as the essentially rejectionist stances of thinkers like Ellul and
Stringfellow.

Yoder sees his work as having two purposes. On the simplest,
most argumentative level it is a restatement of the Christian
pacifist commitment written to protest and refute the various
criticisms of pacifism so prevalent in mainstream theology in
modern times. On the more probing level it is an effort to relate
to ethical matters the "biblical realism" which a generation ago
focused mainly on metaphysical issues. Professing to do so as a
historical theologian rather than as a New Testament scholar,
Yoder examines the New Testament for moral guidance—and
particularly for such moral guidance as can be obtained by taking
very seriously the life and teaching of Jesus and the thinking of
Paul about the powers and the principalities. Yoder feels that the
impact of the New Testament teaching has been blunted by

interpretations based on natural law thinking, realistic theology, and situation ethics—all of which, in different ways, relegate the teachings of Jesus to an incidental significance and turn to alternative standards of action in the political sphere.

Several chapters in the book are concerned with the examination of biblical materials. Yoder boldly challenges traditional readings of many passages in order to show that Jesus intended his teachings to be concretely relevant to a non-violent program of social change. According to Yoder, the cross acquires social significance when seen as a deliberate refusal to conform to the powers of the world. Rejecting as unbiblical understandings of the cross that stress individual experience in apolitical terms, Yoder declares that

> the believer's cross must be, like his Lord's, the price of his social nonconformity. It is not, like sickness or catastrophe, an inexplicable, unpredictable suffering; it is the end of a path freely chosen after counting the cost. It is not, like Luther's or Thomas Müntzer's or Zinzendorf's or Kierkegaard's cross or *Anfechtung*, an inward wrestling of the sensitive soul with self and sin; it is the social reality of representing in an unwilling world the Order to come.[24]

Yoder severely criticizes the choices by which both historical traditionalism and contemporary Christian theology have deflected the revolutionary implications of the teachings of Jesus. These choices include a tendency to ignore the reforming intentions of Jesus in the social situation of his time, the tendency to honor prophets as proclaimers of some ultimate truth while otherwise succumbing to the practical needs of institutional maintenance, the tendency to interiorize the meaning of the Kingdom (which Jesus taught in terms of concrete social change), and a tendency to individualize the message of the Gospel. Yoder is critical of the distinction that was highlighted by Ernst Troeltsch (and that has been dominant in Western theology ever since) to dichotomize between political responsibility and sectarian withdrawal. Such an antithesis between acceptance of political action on the world's terms (which is dubbed "responsible") and the eschewal of politics for the sake of obedience to the Gospel ethics (which is considered to be vocationally pure but socially irrelevant) denies the very concept of Jesus as the Messiah.

Putting his finger adroitly on issues central to this section of our discussion, Yoder indicates the difficulty which is involved even in the vocabulary generally used to discuss the issues.

> It is quite evident in contemporary conversation that one can very well agree on the nature or location of a problem without being sure just how to "get hold of" it. When in modern social analysis such terms as "power" and "structure" are used, everyone knows just about what is meant; but still a logician would have little trouble in demonstrating that not everyone means exactly all the same things and nothing else. Sometimes the term "power" is clearly distinguished from "authority," including in the latter term a special reference to some kind of legitimacy or validation of the exercise of power; other times the two are merged. Sometimes "power" is distinguished from "force" as being somehow more general or more justified or less overt; again they are sometimes identified. The concern for precision and the concern to observe generalities and commonalities constantly cross over and overlap, with linkages being different from every school of thought and every language.[25]

Finding resources in contemporary New Testament scholarship, especially in the writing of H. Berkhof, Yoder suggests that according to the thinking of Paul, the Powers are fallen realities— which means "that they were part of the good creation of God. Society and history, even nature, would be impossible without regularity, system, order—and this need God provided for. The universe is not sustained arbitrarily, immediately, and erratically by an unbroken succession of new divine interventions. It was made in an ordered form and 'it was good.'"[26] Because the Powers were originally created by God, then rebelled and fell because they refused to accept their created (and hence dependent) status and became boasting sources of idolatry, they cannot escape the providential sovereignty of God, who can still use them for good and eventually can redeem them. Just as Jesus subjected himself to the powers of his day, but "morally . . . broke their rules by refusing to support them in their self-glorification,"[27] so the Church must do likewise by being a witness to the liberation accomplished by Christ. Such a strategy can become ". . . in itself a proclamation of the Lordship of Christ to the powers from whose dominion the church has begun to be liberated. The church does not attack the powers; this Christ has done. The church concentrates upon not being seduced by them. By her existence she demonstrates that their rebellion has been vanquished."[28]

Reviewing ecumenical thinking about the responsible society, Yoder accuses it of departing from J. H. Oldham's concern to renew the world from the bottom up, and of opting instead for technical and political approaches that look to a standard quite apart from the Christian witness. This avoids legalistic brittleness but not apostasy.

> In the published documents arising from the ecumenical conversation on social ethics since 1948 there has been a degree of success avoiding the temptations of the Pharisees. There is little tendency to seek to resolve these problems by trusting in some kind of immutable law or loophole-free casuistry. But one cannot be so sure that there has been equal success in discerning and avoiding the temptation of the Sadducees, which is also a form of servitude to the Powers. By this we mean the assumption that the forces which really determine the march of history are in the hand of the leaders of the armies and the markets, in such measure that if Christians are to contribute to the renewal of society they will need to seek, like everyone else—in fact in cooperation with everyone else—to become in their turn the lords of the state and of the economy, so as to use that power toward the ends they consider desirable.[29]

Positively, the church can be said to be called to the role of conscience and servant of society, to pursue the costly role of conscientious objector to the world's way of acting, and to suffer the opposition such objection entails. By proclaiming the Lordship of Christ over the powers, the Church will make known the

concrete relevance of the cross and thus have a new kind of
political impact.

Certain passages in the New Testament, which scholars refer to
as the house rules or house precepts (*Haustafeln*), teach Christians
to be obedient—wives to husbands, children to parents, slaves to
masters, subjects to ruling authorities, etc. Because the early
church moved away from the radical insistence of Jesus that all
the powers had been conquered, these passages came to be interpreted conservatively and they were used to justify subjugation
to established hierarchies. Detailing the difference between the
New Testament passages and the Stoic framework through which
they were wrongly interpreted, Yoder argues that the New
Testament is providing a revolutionary stance in which the
position of subordination is given a different moral meaning. In
the new Testament, the passages call for the dominant partner in
each case to accept a kind of subordination in service just as the
subordinate partner accepts a fidelity in service. This is a revolutionary call rather than an affirmation of the order of creation.

> For a first-century husband to love (*agapan*) his wife or for a
> first-century father to avoid angering his child, or for a first-
> century master to deal with his servant in the awareness that
> they are both slaves to a higher master, is to make a more
> concrete and more sweeping difference in the way that husband
> or father or master behaves than the other imperative of subor-
> dination would have made practically in the behavior of the
> wife or child or servant.[30]

In a curious disclaimer at the end of the chapter on revolutionary
subordination, Yoder declares that the principle he has enunciated
is an analysis of where the New Testament offered specific
guidance for its time, not an overall social ethic for dealing with
modern issues. But in contrast to Ellul, and perhaps even to
Stringfellow, Yoder has far more urgency to show the relevance
of his position to the way we live—a much greater relevance than
is traditionally assumed in his own Mennonite tradition of non-
resistance to evil.

The concept of power against which Ellul, Stringfellow, and Yoder protest is a common one in Western thought, if not indeed the controlling one. Bernard M. Loomer, in the first D. R. Sharpe lecture at the University of Chicago Divinity School, spoke of it as "unilateral power"—the ability to produce intended or desired effects by influencing, guiding, manipulating, shaping, controlling or transforming the human or material environment for one's own benefit and by one's own actions. It is non-mutual; one-sided, it involves power *over* that which is dealt with. It dominates in sports and, as in zero sum competition, requires the gain of one to be had at the loss of another. This view of power is non-relational; it makes self-sufficiency axiomatic; it thinks of freedom as inhering in the autonomy of the self—not as derived from society. It is power of the kind that Reinhold Niebuhr warned becomes inordinate and Lord Acton said corrupts.

A second concept of power, which Loomer calls relational power, involves the ability both to produce and to undergo an effect, both to influence and to allow oneself to be influenced. It involves mutuality, the strengthening that comes from being related to others. Instead of the capacity only to produce an effect, it involves the capacity to sustain a mutually enriching relation, a capacity to transcend inequalities. Relational power seeks to create groups of larger and larger size and diversity rather than groups that exclude all except those of the same interest. It seeks to overcome conflict and violence, to use the ambiguities that inhere in all human relationships for creative growth. It sees in Jesus a paradigm which, while at the bottom of the hierarchy in terms of unilateral power, "stands at the apex of life conceived in terms of relational power."[31] While it is possible to have a reasonably well-ordered society (in the institutional sense) by exercising unilateral power, the exercise of relational power allows repressed forces to surface, roles to be transformed, and crises to be resolved. Only by opening up human possibilities in this way can a new kind of human existence emerge.

Loomer's treatment has fascinating parallels to the orientation of the gospel intentionalists but its framework of discourse is process theology and a general analysis of human experience. It may not be as suspicious of worldly possibilities, as assertive of the uniqueness of the Gospel imperatives, but it is just as insistent that something very different has to emerge if human life is to become more human.

Many American Christians who respond to Jacques Ellul and his thinking are involved in intentional forms of Christian community. Will D. Campbell, director of the Committee of Southern Churchmen, is one of the most articulate.[32] He argues against social action, politics, and even education because cooperation with them results in accommodation to, rather than the transformation of, humanity. The proclamation of the new life which we have in Christ should take the form of feeding the hungry, clothing the naked, visiting the sick, and similar acts of compassion and charity. Disillusioned with an early career in parish ministry, social action, and college chaplaincy—all of which involved support of "Caesar's institutions," Campbell came to see that all views that separate people into "we/they" dichotomies fail to embody the realization that in Jesus Christ all have been reconciled.

Another group whose thought and action demonstrates the intentionalist way of dealing with society publishes the magazine *Sojourners*.[33] The People's Christian Coalition, consisting of evangelical Christians from many kinds of vocational activity, seeks to serve the Lord through sacrificial living and with service patterned on the earliest doctrines, practices, and revolutionary impulses of Christianity. Much Christian intentionalism in the past fifteen years has come from similar evangelical orientations.[34]

This concludes the account of those thinkers, trends, and movements that, between 1965 and 1980, relate to the six motifs developed in *A Survey of Christian Ethics*. The form of the motifs is quite as discernible now as it was when they were first suggested, though the tendency to argue for the exclusive necessity of one is much softened for those motifs dealing with the formulation of the ethical norm and a bit sharpened for those dealing with the implementation of the ethical decision. But certain other developments must be taken into account to give an adequate picture of Christian ethics during the last fifteen years. Considerable attention has been given to moral agency and to different frameworks which have arisen to affect the ways in which Christian ethics is approached. The rest of this study explores those matters.

III

Moral Agency

7

Attention to Virtue and Character

The concept of moral discernment, which in Chapter 1 was examined in relation to moral reasoning, also refers to a certain quality of character, or personal moral ability, which involves dispositions, traits, and skills of the moral agent rather than the conclusions about normative judgments to which a person comes. When, in discussing moral discernment, James Gustafson writes about the "moral clod" and the "moral virtuoso," he goes beyond the particular moral judgments which individuals make. He is talking about qualities of their being, or character. In Christian terms, he is referring to "fundamental dispositions that are shaped in part by the faith and trust Christians have as they offer themselves up to God."[1] Such language points beyond moral reasoning and its conclusions to affective sensibilities and to qualities of personal being.

There is an increasing interest among Christian ethicists in the significance of the character of the moral agent and in the question as to how the kind of person one is bears upon the kind of decisions one makes. Attention to virtues, certainly not new in Christian ethics, has again become an important focus of attention. Gustafson advances the discussion of these matters in his book, *Can Ethics Be Christian?* by considering the bearing of "the 'sort of person' one is" on moral decision. Factors such as character type, life-style, motivation, and the quality of personhood that shape predictably consistent responses, become central to ethical inquiry. It is not enough to arrive at conceptual clarity concerning norms. We must inquire how we can come to be certain kinds of persons.

According to this approach, the capacity to hope, the capacity to be faithful, and the capacity to love can be understood more adequately as virtues than as norms. In pointing to these Gustafson is modest concerning the extent to which a Christian commitment results in a transformation of the self at the deep subconscious levels. He recognizes that it is often difficult to pin-point the formative influences which shape people's values and outlooks, and particularly difficult to trace the extent to which religious influences are determinative in the lives, not only of those who profess but even of those who do not consciously hold to a religious outlook. "It is plausible to claim, however, not only that religious communities tend to form persons with certain preferences for values, including moral values, but also that a conscious awareness of the reality of God, a living of a life of faith, can alter the values that persons have come to hold."[2]

The second half of the book *Christian Ethics and the Community* contains several essays by Gustafson dealing with the moral virtues. In reference to character, he observes in the first of these essays, that

> in ordinary moral life, we come to expect that certain people will fairly consistently act in certain ways. Under similar circumstances they will do similar things; their choices seem to be in part predictable, and thus there appears to be an implicit if not explicit consistency in the values to which they are loyal; their motives, insofar as one can judge them, appear not to be erratic, but to persist through different experiences and different actions. Indeed, a great deal of ordinary moral action relies upon the reliability of others; it is predicated upon some degree of predictability of the behavior of others. We assume that there are some relatively stable characteristics in ourselves, and in the selfhoods of others. Indeed, we rely upon persons to have certain characters.[3]

The task of ethics, Gustafson suggests, includes coming to understand character and its importance to the moral tasks of the community. This leads us to recognize some relationship between a person's temperament and the standards, norms, rules, and principles that person professes. It leads us to examine in what frames of reference, i.e. associational patterns of fidelity and interaction, a person lives, and how these are operative in an individual's life. It involves the examination of certain inner psychic orientations that are internalized in a given individual. It involves the development of a more adequate theory for understanding the ways in which personal communities are related to impersonal ones, for those forms of Christian ethics that sharply dichotomize the personal element from the social element ignore the fact that "the well-being of the group, and of its individual member, requires that certain values be adhered to, whether one has a bureaucracy in view or whether one has a 'fellowship' in view."[4]

Raising considerations in much the same manner as does Gustafson, Tom L. Beauchamp and James F. Childress, having devoted seven chapters in *The Principles of Biomedical Ethics*[5] to the interplay of theories, principles, rules, and particular decisions, devote a concluding chapter to ideals, virtues, and integrity. This concluding chapter considers more directly the qualities needed in the health professional as a moral agent. It examines, with reference to a work by J. O. Urmson,[6] the nature of heroic and saintly actions, in which people do more than required by duty because of some special quality to their lives. Turning to the examination of the relation of acts to virtues, Beauchamp and Childress acknowledge the interrelationship but refuse to grant the primacy of either over the other. They particularly object to the view that the presence of good motives alone (as these would be present in a caring professional) can ensure that the actions of that individual will be moral. Even persons of fine character can make bad decisions. "While many virtues such as modesty, patience, promptness, and fearlessness, have had a place in medical codes, the most important moral virtues correlate with the major principles and rules of ethics as applied to medical practice. These include, but are not limited to, veracity, benevolence (including nonmalevolence), respect for persons (particularly their autonomy), and justice."[7]

The addition of the concluding chapter on the character of the health professional in a volume on the principles of bio-medical ethics indicates a growing awareness of the importance that is coming to be attached to the quality of the moral agent.

A similar shift of nuance can be observed in the thinking of Bernard Häring. In *The Law of Christ*,[8] published in the 1960s, the focus is on normative considerations. In the more recent *Free and Faithful in Christ*, Häring has a good deal to say about the nature of the ethical person. "Moral theology is interested," he writes, "not only in decisions and actions. It raises the question, 'What ought I to do?' but asks, first of all, 'What ought I to be: what kind of person does the Lord want me to be?'"[9] Häring disapproves the tendency of modern ethicists to dispense with the term "virtue" and examines some of the substitutes that have been employed, such as "pattern," "posture," or "character."

Häring's own terminology, which is "fundamental disposition," is closely related to the term "fundamental option." Fundamental option "is an intention that has at least the dynamics of being all-pervasive in the orientation and quality of all one's free decisions and actions."[10] It bears the normative element, to which the behavioral aspects are related.

> When one's fundamental option so permeates one's inner self that it becomes a fundamental attitude, new intuitions and new dispositions arise. There develops a lasting tendency to think, desire and act in such a way that the person becomes trustworthy, and there can be no doubt about his or her identity or character.[11]

Häring stresses an essential relationship between the fundamental option and the fundamental disposition, but he sees the virtues as flowing from the acknowledged norms and not the other way around. Granting that virtue is related to disposition, Häring remains suspicious of any effort to ground morality in dispositions alone. Hence he says, "We can conceive virtues as specific attitudes in response to particular spheres of values."[12]

> Although a meaningful renewal of our intention, along with renewal of concrete purposes, might be useful and frequently necessary, the moral and religious value of our acts can reach the highest level only when the fundamental option so pervades our vision and our energies that the pure motives and important decisions arise spontaneously from the depth in which the Spirit moulds and guides us.[13]

Robert O. Johann has given us still another discussion of Christian ethics that includes a significant place for the concept of virtue and concern about the character and quality of the moral agent. He contends that both sides in the debate between "principles" and "situations" overlooked the importance of the ideas of habit, virtue, and character. Situationalism overlooked the importance of these factors because it did not give sufficient attention to the whole odyssey of the moral agent, which has so shaped itself through a series of responses to events in the past as to set up dispositional tendencies (habits, if you will) that do function determinatively in handling emerging issues. "Both the sort of agent I have been and the sort of agent I am to be—that is, the whole question of character—is involved in every decision."[14] The advocates of rule morality (and, by inference those who use principles as action guides) focus attention upon the norms rather than on the agency.

In his book *The Meaning of Love* Johann makes reference neither to character nor to virtue as central rubrics, but he does set forth a concept of love that involves a thoroughgoing appreciation of the place of interiority in its realization, as well as the importance of relating that interiority to both others and the Other. This framework, which is not uncongenial to a relational approach, does provide a perspective from which Johann can develop views about the importance of character. Certainly the perspective is implicit in this concluding paragraph.

Thus man's destiny is ultimately not a pursuit but an unfolding. His goal is not a fragment on the horizon, but a God on whose fullness he draws. His basic choice is not what good to acquire, but what orientation to assume. Will he be attentive to the presence of Being? Will he respond to the presence of the Infinite? Only by answering the gift of the Self with the gift of himself can he ever fully and consciously be what he is. Only by animating the torrential multiplicity of his desires with the fire of a single love—a love whose term is ultimately more himself than he is himself—can he realize fully and consciously in his own life that interiority and adhesion to Being in which he participates, and that communion with Being to which he is called. Only by digging deep into the value of the self will he break through to paradise.[15]

Viewing character as "the personal achievement of a stable and fruitful relationship with one's natural and social environment,"[16] Johann argues that it can look to the concrete without being lost in immediacy and can also be responsive to normative considerations without creating externalized erosions of freedom. In short, an approach that stresses the role of character in Christian thinking "stresses what contemporary moralists so often forget, that moral goodness is primarily a perfection of persons, not of acts; that actions are good only in relation to the goodness of person; that this goodness of persons is a matter of habitual dispositions that have to be worked at to be acquired."[17]

A similar effort to portray an ethics of character and virtue as a middle way between principled and situational approaches has been mounted by Stanley Hauerwas, who has developed this position much more extensively and in a somewhat more polemical fashion. Indeed, Hauerwas may well have been one of the persons Beauchamp and Childress had in mind when they deliberately disassociated themselves from "those (a) who try to drive a wedge between an ethics of duty and an ethics of virtue or between acts and agents, or (b) who try to make the ethics of virtue primary."[18] For Hauerwas the concept of virtue and attention to the importance of character are much more central than, even decisively prior to, the normative. While Hauerwas does not see this emphasis as making a break with the main aspects of the past, he does contend that it is a decisive modification of much recent reflection. Hauerwas holds that situationalism puts the emphasis on the same place as the approaches against which it has developed, namely, upon the encounters in life where decisions have to be made rather than upon the agents who have to make the decision. Because all participants in the debate precipitated by situation ethics argue whether or not the responsible moral life consists of conformity to rule or sensitivity to the complexities of situations they tend to forget "that what is at stake in most of our decisions is not the act itself, but the kind of person we will be."[19]

Hauerwas proposes an approach in which the moral notions of the agent have more fundamental consequences than they have in the thinking of the situationalists. Attention is directed to the moral notions of the agent rather than to the decisions that agent should make. "The moral life is not first a life of choice—decision is not king—but is rather woven from the notions that we use to see and to form the situations we confront. Moral life involves learning to see the world through an imaginative ordering of our basic symbols and notions."[20] The redirection of attention that is involved means that we do morals more as the artist encounters his work than as the critic who subsequently makes an analytical or evaluative judgment about the work of the artist.

Moral notions cannot take the form of prima facie norms—about this Hauerwas would say Joseph Fletcher is right. Reflective analysis does not rise above the indefiniteness and ambiguity present in reality, and only insofar as we bring forth from within ourselves a vision which shapes the world can we hope to develop an adequate ethic. Putting the attention on vision rather than on choice takes attention away from adherence to universalizable rules and requires that we become concerned with "our experiences, fables, beliefs, images, concepts and inner monologues."[21] Freedom, for instance, comes to be understood, not so much as a capacity to enact whatever decision of the will we come to in response either to rules or to contexts, but a power to see things more creatively, to recognize others with equality and fairness, and to have a selfless respect for reality.

Hauerwas develops both a conceptualization of the idea of

character and an epistemology to sustain it. His formal definition of character is, succinctly put, "the qualification of man's self-agency through his beliefs, intentions, and actions, by which a man acquires a moral history befitting his nature as a self-determining being."[22] This definition points to the ways in which individuals manage their given personal dispositions, the degree of consistency they manifest in doing so, and the manner of their responses. It refers also to the pattern of experiences and the quality of responses that any individual has demonstrated and may reasonably be expected to continue to demonstrate. The idea of character involves not only qualities in the moral agent but also the communities to which the moral agent has been related and from which he draws norms, values and directions.

The idea of agency, which attributes some degree of power to a person to change surrounding circumstances as well as one's own behavior, is central to the idea of character. To be sure, the concept can be made so simplistic as to overlook destiny—or that aspect of experience that seems more given than cultivated. It can also be oversimplified in ways that obscure the fact that we do some things in a less than voluntary way (such as perspiring) or without any conscious purpose (such as randomly crossing a street). Even so, the "qualification of the self-agency" points to the fact that "we are who we are because we can form our action, and thus ourselves, as we envision and choose courses of behavior."[23] We are continually determining our behavior by relating the intentions and beliefs we hold to the experiences to which we respond, with the result that there is both a private and a public dimension to our selfhood, a sense in which we are both active and passive in relation to experience, a sense in which there is both continuity and change involved in our being what we are.

According to Hauerwas, being moral is fundamentally more a process of learning to see the world in a particular way than it is a process of enunciating principles. The views of Hauerwas and Häring differ sharply on this point, for in Häring the norms shape the character whereas in Hauerwas the character has primary influence on the norms. Moreover, for Hauerwas, an epistemology that makes use of vision and a discourse set forth in story is more useful for ethics than analytical scrutiny and the statement of principles and logical relationships. "The moral life does not consist just in making one right decision after another; it is the progressive attempt to widen and clarify our vision of reality."[24] It is not solely a matter of doing, but of seeing and hearing. Seeing and hearing depend upon metaphor and vision more than on rules and principles.

The foregoing discussions pose a question whether the priorities of ethics lie with a determination of norms or the cultivation of character. They may suggest that there has been (or may be) an obligations/virtue debate as polarizing as the norms/context debate. But the likelihood that such will occur seems doubtful. In 1973 the *Journal of Religious Ethics*[25] printed several articles dealing with the relation of virtue and obligation in religious ethics. All of these articles examined the differences that arise when ethics is looked at from one or the other of these poles, and one of them even spoke about "the virtue-obligation controversy." But everyone of these articles resisted making a sharp dichotomy between these two approaches.

If it has been the case that some ethicists, particularly those strongly neo-Reformation Protestants whose formulations dominated the period lasting two or three decades following World War II, neglected the place of virtue and the role of character in Christian thinking, then the current treatment is a helpful corrective. But Roman Catholic thinking, which is increasingly important to all of us, made no such de-emphasis, and as any student of Jonathan Edwards knows, American Protestants could neglect the importance of virtue only by being oblivious to aspects of their own heritage. Even Immanuel Kant, that stern advocate of duty and imperatives, stressed that fidelity to the norm produces a new kind of personal orientation which he called a change of heart. Nor can some of the more substantial books published at the same time these discussions were going on be understood as taking sides in a contrast posed in this fashion. Daniel D. Williams, in *The Spirit and the Forms of Love*,[26] makes little of the distinction, and what he says about love could not be encompassed by either side of the distinction by itself.

Meanwhile, something can be said for having the virtues described. One book that does this effectively is Romano Guardini's *The Virtues: On Forms of Moral Life.* Guardini informs us that as early as 1955 the philosopher Max Scheler was attempting to rehabilitate the idea of virtue as a corrective for Kant's emphasis on duties, and Guardini's own contribution consists less of arguing the theory than exploring the meaning of the virtues. The list of them is a long one; truthfulness, acceptance, patience, justice, reverence, loyalty, disinterestedness, asceticism, courage, kindness, understanding, courtesy, gratitude, unselfishness, recollection, silence, and justice before God. Guardini, in speaking about justice, moves directly from the personal to the corporate level.

> Everyone should say to himself: the history of nations moves in the same way as the affairs in my home. The state mirrors the way in which I order my small sphere of action. All criticism should begin with ourselves, and with the intention of improving things. Then we would soon see how much goes wrong because we do not permit the other person to be who he is and do not give him the room which he requires.[27]

It is also possible to deal with character in terms of traits to be avoided rather than in terms of those to be cultivated. William F. May has done this in *A Catalogue of Sins: A Contemporary Examination of Christian Conscience.* He reacts less against an ethic of obligation than against a theology that speaks powerfully against sin but does not deal adequately with the concrete and particular forms in which character is assaulted. His list of sins includes false worship; false fear; false mastery; envy, hatred, neglect of the needy; betrayal, lust, deceit, craving and anxiety, pride and sloth. Each of these is examined in an individual chapter and in a manner which focuses less on "the *faculties* a man possesses than with the *situations* in which he finds himself."[28] With this orientation May maintains attention on the social framework of sins, which in turn suggests a social framework for conscience.

The discussion of virtue as an ingredient in moral thinking will probably be with us for some time as an important emphasis, as a corrective when called for, within a broader treatment of the moral life. It does have an important bearing on ethics and prompts a closer examination of how moral agents function and what can be done to enhance their moral capability. Attention to these concerns also involves the examination of the role and functioning of conscience, which is the object of attention in the next chapter.

8

Analyses of Conscience

Ethicists have often spoken of conscience, though the meaning of the term has been subject to different understandings and the function of conscience a matter of debate. Moreover, in recent years the moral faculties have been studied by psychologists, students of Christian nurture, and those concerned with pastoral theology. Discussions between the scholars in these disciplines and ethicists are developing and creating bridge-conversations that supplement those which already exist between ethics and philosophy and between ethics and the social sciences.

Just as Kant was pivotal for thinking about moral reasoning, so Freud was pivotal for thinking about moral agency in psychological terms. He raised questions that still influence the discussion of conscience and still are central in the contemporary situation. His challenges, among them one to the popular idea of conscience as a nagging voice creating a sense of guilt about naughty acts, form issues even for those who reject his conclusions.

Eric Mount's book *Conscience and Responsibility* considers the role that conscience plays in the lives of contemporary persons— a role that continues to be acknowledged in everyday responses even if its validity is questioned by theoretical discussions and has been neglected in some recent Protestant thought. It argues for a recasting of our thinking about conscience to take into account the developments in psychology, sociology, and philosophy that have occurred since traditional views of conscience were functional in Western thought, but not necessarily to succumb to the judgments these seem to require.

Looking at the challenges to the traditional views of conscience raised by post-Freudian thinkers and by secular experience, Mount suggests that both the inner and outer references of the self must be examined in any adequate account of moral agency. Concern for the outer reference, which looks at institutional and communal aspects of morality, was well nurtured in Protestant liberalism, whereas many forms of neo-orthodoxy focused attention on the inner dimensions. The time is ripe for a fuller synthesis.

> Almost all Christian ethicists today largely realize the impossibility of separating the self and its communities. When the spotlight is on the moral agent, the culture of the self cannot be left in darkness. When issues of civil rights and international relations are the focal concern, these cannot be considered in isolation from an understanding of the structures of prejudice and the way man's immorality takes peculiar forms in his immoral societies. Whether the focus is inner or outer, the concerns must always be inclusive rather than exclusive. A renewed concern with conscience has had to reflect this realization. Conscience cannot be legitimately reduced either to an inner or an outer matter, either to social pressure or to a solitary sense. Neither individual independence or social engineering holds the key to understanding the Christian moral agent. The self and his societies must be considered together.[1]

Mount chides rationalistic, voluntaristic, and emotive reductionisms that set conscience apart from the totality of the self or explain it away naturalistically. He points to the limitations involved in understanding conscience only as the accuser. He criticizes popularized versions of the Freudian perspective, in which conscience is portrayed merely as a super ego intrusion intensifying repression. In contrast to these views he finds guide-posts to a more adequate conception of moral authority in a variety of thinkers—in Gordon Allport's contention that the mature religious person is "ought" directed instead of "must" directed; in Brian Moore's literary portrayal of an Irish youth in whom a personal capacity to take responsibility for decisions replaces imagined instruction from a white angel on one shoulder and a black angel on the other shoulder; in James Lapsley's discussion of the difference between a "guilt dynamic" and a "shame dynamic"; and in Stuart Hampshire's conceptualization of character as the pattern of the self's established habits of action.

Mount then works through the concept of conscience in a number of Christian theologians, suggesting them to be most on target when thinking, to use Paul Lehmann's terminology, of conscience as "the total self's response from within the nexus of the Christian fellowship to the humanizing action of God."[2] Similar perspectives can be discerned, Mount argues, in the thought of Dietrich Bonhoeffer, Helmut Thielieke, Gerhard Ebeling, and H. Richard Niebuhr. Rethinking of these matters can also be found in Roman Catholic moral theologians like Bernard Häring and Charles Curran. The Roman Catholics, like the Protestants, stress conscience in terms of the total self, but they tend to be a little clearer with specific guidance. Some "fleeting references" to contemporary (non-Christian) thought are used by Mount to supplement his movement toward a holistic concept. Buber's social existentialism, Erikson's psycho-analytical theory, Wittgenstein's opposition to the idea of a "soul inside the body," and Arendt's insistence that sociality is the fundamental nature of the human condition, all play roles in Mount's effort at reconceptualization.

Mount develops the dual relationship between conscience and responsibility with reference both to H. Richard Niebuhr's sense of dialectic between the self and the other, and to Gerhard Ebeling's idea of man's co-humanity with man. Both thinkers see the whole self reflected in conscience rather than conscience as a special thing possessed by the self. Mount's own view, which emerges in responsive appreciation from the common elements in these quite different thinkers, involves internalized elements ("oughts," integral selfhood, etc.) and externalized elements ("musts," submission to others for the sake of social adjustment, etc.). It can be expressed in both deontological obedience to obligation and in teleological striving toward an ideal, and it involves (as H. Richard Niebuhr sensed) the center of value that gives the self its ultimate worth and purpose as well as the social context in relation to which the individual lives and acts.

> Integrity then is not individualistic but relational. If a person hear Thoreau's "different drummer" contradicting a society of which he is a part, he may be responding to a community rather than a crowd, but his conscience is still in some sense social. The laws and goals which his conscience defends grow out of personal relations. The self reaches beyond itself and beyond the conscience of the community, but what it reaches toward has invariably been pointed to if not achieved or exhausted in one of its communities.[3]

After setting forth these initial definitions of conscience, Mount turns to a variety of issues and situations. He looks at the changing dimensions of community authority, at concepts of sin and salvation, at obedience to Jesus Christ as a moral model, at the Christian *koinonia* as a context for decision-making, and at the issues between ethics of guidance (norms) and those of context. Mount makes a significant place in his thinking for community in its institutionalized expressions, for reconciliation to God despite our sin, and for the church as a fellowship in which moral choices are surrounded by structured frameworks of identity and expectation. Speaking of the tension between the prescriptive quality of rules and the claims of circumstances, Mount declares it is possible to respond to a living God by taking due note of the generalizations, patterns, and characteristic elements that make a Christian life style, while at the same time being creatively spontaneous and exercising the freedom to deal with particular circumstances in the Christian life. Near the end of his discussion Mount makes this summarizing definition of conscience:

The Christian conscience then is a knowing with one-self or an integrity of heart in which the self's integrity or image of itself is constituted in God as he has made himself and true manhood known in Jesus Christ and as this revelation is mediated through the Christian community. The joint authorship of conscience, i.e., the self-in-the-Christian-community and the Christian-community-in-the-self, points to and is derived from a transcendent theonomous authority. Because the God to whom man is ultimately accountable is known in Christ as friend, his judgment is known to be gracious. In sin, by contrast, the self attempts to have its own independent conscience or makes some other center of value besides God its authority. Conscience as sinful is then legalistic, libertine, or idolatrous instead of covenantal or reconciled to God.[4]

As a religious educator, Carl Ellis Nelson has been consistently concerned with the relation of the nurture of faith to the growth of moral capability. His book *Where Faith Begins* examines the role of the community of believers in the development of faith and seeks a more viable place for the church in shaping the controlling values of those who profess Christianity. In the preface to this book he takes note of the terrible strain on conventional ethical codes created by the present cultural climate and predicts that strain will intensify in the future. "There is no question," he writes, "that conscience must be constantly refurbished to meet new conditions which were not in existence when conscience was formed in the present adult population a generation earlier."[5]

Nelson is aware how difficult it is to deal with ethical issues as congregational matters. The underlying individualism that considers moral decisions to be private is deeply pervasive. Those who belong to contemporary local congregations would be nonplussed to have such congregations judge their behavior, even though they will tolerate the enunciation of moral ideals from the pulpit. Nelson notes the irony in the fact that people often discuss moral problems in other contexts, but cease to do so when they are in the church. He contends that the home—which is often assumed to bear the burden of moral formation—would be greatly helped if the Christian congregation was more functional in dealing with ethical issues.

In a chapter discussing "Faith and Values" Nelson tackles the problem of conscience, which he contends "is one of the most important areas for practical theology to investigate."[6] We know relatively little about the development or the functioning of conscience even though it is a very powerful regulator of human conduct. Nelson contends that values develop out of social interaction, and that the current cultural situation is one of change and fluidity rather than of stability and continuity— which makes value formation difficult. Much of his discussion is devoted to ways to interpret the moral understandings of the Bible without lifting concepts and normative formulations devised in one epoch into another apart from the necessary historical transposition. "[Christians] must analyze the human situation they face in relation to similar situations in the Bible in order to judge whether the Biblical affirmations apply to the contemporary situation or whether they must develop new values."[7]

Shortly after the publication of *Where Faith Begins*, with its indications that moral concerns are closely intertwined with growth in religious faith, Nelson brought together a series of selections, many of which were chosen from other books and some from journals, dealing with the nature and function of conscience as understood by both theological and psychological observers.[8] This tool for teaching and reflection—which is useful because it brings into one place comments from many sources upon the nature of conscience, was followed about four years later by a small and preliminary effort to describe and evaluate the nature of conscience in light of both theological tradition and attempts of social scientists to describe the varieties and stages of moral development. Nelson's book has a catchy title,[9] but its message is intensely serious though admittedly preliminary.[10] Nelson identifies the experiences of anxiety and hostility that are involved in the human odyssey, notes the traditional view (expressed with greatest abandon in Protestantism) that conscience is the voice of God within the individual, and he suggests the need to be wary of viewing conscience as a simplistic source of guidance standing over or against, above or beyond, the self. "The capacity to develop a conscience is," he argues, "innate, but the content of conscience will come from society."[11] The early training of the child, both from parents and experience, develops certain internally felt regulations that are restrictive and produce feelings of guilt if violated. This view of conscience, despite its widespread prevalence in the history of Christianity, is a negative one and needs to be reconsidered in light of what we now understand to be a more adequate pattern of human development. It develops from training—even training of a type that inculcates response patterns in animals. It has social origins and differs in content from culture to culture. It is nurtured through the processes by which the young child identifies with parents. Conscience, particularly in this negative form, creates feelings of guilt when strictures are transgressed. Guilt often leads to various psychological responses—self-punishment, partial restitution, denial, habitual use of ritual, scapegoating, and the transfer of responsibility to the social group.

There are four kinds of behavior among religious persons that may be latent ways of dealing with the negative conscience. One is to profess belief in God without letting one's life be touched by his demands; another is to wallow in the subjective side of the doctrine of forgiveness; a third is to pursue moral goodness with a fierce intensity; and a fourth is to engage in a specious casuistry —make the moral law lifeless and dull instead of vibrant and inspiring. In contrast to the negative conscience, a positive set of goals, which Nelson calls the "positive conscience," can be developed. Whereas violations of the negative conscience produce guilt, violations of the positive conscience produce shame. Shame can be handled differently than guilt and can have creative consequences in guiding persons to do God's will.

When we become mature persons a conversation takes place with ourselves about "the kind of person we want to be in relation to the people and things around us."[12] While the process of establishing ego-certainty is ethically neutral, and may occur in those who become anti-social as well as in those who become social, an understanding of that process is nevertheless crucial if we are to achieve maturity in the moral self. Nelson turns to Erik

Erikson's contours of moral development and cites the importance of basic trust for understanding faith. While Erikson brackets the issue as to whether belief in God is essential to having trust, Nelson asserts that Christian faith, maturely held, furnishes a way of achieving valid independence from culturally enslaving repressions. All parts of the self are affected and thus a psychological wholeness becomes functional to faith, though by no means the equivalent of faith. Faith goes beyond mere wholeness of the self to engender compassion even for those "who have little social power or respectability and for people who cannot be expected to return the feeling of compassion."[13] Nelson concludes by examining the healthy and the unhealthy ways in which religious faith can be embraced and shows how a healthy faith is essential for a healthy moral agency.

The discussion of conscience found in Donald E. Miller's book *The Wing-Footed Wanderer: Conscience and Transcendence* begins with the history of the idea of conscience in the Western tradition, an examination of the attacks made in post-Freudian thinking upon the reliability of conscience, and examines at some length the implications for the understanding of conscience present in moral development theories. His book is something of a bridge-discussion between the concerns of this chapter and those of the next. We will have things to say about it in both.

Miller considers Freud's essentially negative understanding of conscience as an accusing entity that generates guilt, and he points out that those who would argue for a constructive model of conscience must take Freud seriously. By taking Freud seriously, and most particularly by acknowledging the debilitating consequences of conscience considered as "restrictive, repressive, self-destructive and infantile,"[14] we should be spurred to develop a more positive description of moral judgment—a description that can undergird freely chosen directions and purposes. Turning to Erik Erikson's views of the moral self, under the rubric of "the sponsoring conscience," Miller shows how the Harvard psychologist was able to utilize those emotive elements that contribute to moral health while remaining informed by, and appreciative of, Freud's insights. Erikson's understanding of moral development (epigenesis) holds that certain stages must be completed, and in a fixed and identifiable order, as human beings develop morally. Moral experience stems from interactional encounters with other human beings, and these account for the development of hope, will, purpose, competence, love, care, and integrity. Erikson's thinking about the emergence of moral and ethical aspects of the person as an individual matures interprets the super-ego "not only as a source of aggression and rage against the ego, [but as that which] also preserves the sense of self-worth."[15] In adolescence the person searches, sometimes by trial and error (and basically in relation to others) for a new identity, in which one becomes at one with oneself, one's community and one's historical epoch. The "sponsoring conscience" that results from overcoming repressive moralism includes "fidelity to what one is in his own group and in his own time."[16] The development of conscience continues into adult life and reaches maturity when the ego learns to love. Summarizing Erikson's understandings of these matters, Miller points to four qualities of ego strength that are present when the moral agent is free and mature: "1) spontaneous expression not controlled by unconscious defenses, perceptual distortion, or ideology; 2) strong volition and intentionality; 3) conscious, rational deliberation and choice with constantly revised and renewed coherence of experience, meaning, purpose, and ideals; and 4) mutuality between persons, institutions, and events such that each enhances all and all enhance each."[17] This view of conscience presupposes a view of human affairs that believes it is possible for such affairs to be governed by reason and marked by mutuality. While the powerful cultural forces thwarting the culmination of such a moral maturity in persons cannot be denied, the struggle to move toward it is worthwhile.

The last chapter of Miller's book, which discusses conscience in relation to transcendence, reveals his community of concern with those in the psychoanalytic tradition who feel that a censorial and repressive conscience is unhealthy. Miller repeatedly contrasts ways in which certain embraces of religious duty weaken human agency while other forms of religious aspiration enhance the possibilities of creative response. The risk-venture of open response is crucial, and efforts to be altogether certain or altogether righteous are enemies of both psychological and religious health. Reading this chapter leaves little doubt that if forced to choose between restrictive, repressive, and authoritarian modes of religious obedience and free, open, trusting, and integrated responsiveness as envisioned by psychologists (more constructively by Piaget and Erikson than by Freud) Miller would opt for the second. But he contends we do not need to choose, that we can have religious faith and a helpful conscience within the parameters of freedom and openness. Miller recognizes that not all religious people know this, as the presence of tyrants and inquisitors who have strafed others in their zeal to guarantee righteousness for God shows. "We may recognize the misuse of references to God's righteousness, but our response is to be with a deeper awareness, a larger sense of purpose, greater coherence in relation to the circumstances, and with a deeper sense of being one with those to whom our attention is given."[18]

The foregoing accounts of conscience generally seek a concept of moral sensitivity that affirms individual and social values. Appreciative of the main trends in psychoanalysis since Freud, these accounts argue the need to move beyond the repressive forms of conscience associated with traditional religious views. Our account of contemporary thinking about conscience would not be complete without considering a group of books in which more traditional formulations about the ideas of sin and guilt are set forth. Karl Menninger may have started the recent exploration of these matters in his 1973 book with the provocative title *Whatever Became of Sin?* Sketching that plethora of problems confronting modern industrial societies, Menninger remarks,

> The very word "sin," which seems to have disappeared, was a proud word. It was once a strong word, an ominous and serious word. It described a central point in every civilized human being's life plan and life style. But the word went away. It has almost disappeared—the word, along with the notion.[19]

Menninger contends that modern society has largely let the idea of sin suffer eclipse—indeed, at one time he had "even joined in hailing its going."[20] This eclipse has several dimensions. In one, sin is relegated to the periphery of modern consciousness by reinterpreting it as "crime" (responsibility for punishing which is a civil rather than a religious matter and is being horrendously botched in contemporary America); in a second, sin is treated as a symptom of a disease (thus declaring it to be involuntary and beyond culpability—in need of therapy instead of punishment); in a third, it is treated as a consequence of collective behavior (which transfers responsibility for wrongdoing to the group and protects both leader and other members of the group from having to face adverse information about their behavior). In discussing these ways of masking the reality of sin, Menninger hardly comforts the traditional defenders of law and order or conventional morality. His condemnations of social repression, of the criminal justice system's penchant for punishment, of American's rape of the land, robbery of the Indians, onetime tolerance of institutional slavery and present acquiescence to economic slavery, easy acquiescence in war and preparation for it, are hardly the stuff of which right-wing moral crusades are compounded. His effort to refurbish the idea of sin bears no similarity to the calls for the defense of privilege sometimes touted as the defense of morality. "The moralistic bullyboys are no friends or allies of mine . . . they are wrong. But they are not concerned with sin. They are not concerned with morality, only with legality and vengeance."[21]

Menninger examines the list of seven deadly sins—envy, anger, pride, sloth, avarice, gluttony, and lust. He gives each a modern interpretation. He adds several new sins to the list: affluence, wastefulness, cheating and stealing, lying, cruelty, and callousness to the psychic well-being of others.

> My proposal is for the revival or reassertion of personal responsibility in all human acts, good and bad. Not total responsibility, but not zero either. I believe that all evildoing in which we become involved to any degree tends to evoke guilt feelings and depression. These may or may not be clearly

perceived, but they affect us. They may be reacted to and covered up by all kinds of escapism, rationalization, and re-action or symptom formation. To revive the half-submerged idea of personal responsibility and to seek appropriate measures of reparation might turn the tide of our aggressions and of the moral struggle in which much of the world population is engaged.[22]

To achieve this result Menninger argues that guilt must be openly acknowledged (confessed) and expiated (atoned for) by restitution and revised behavior. He pleads for a movement away from Augustine's stress of the inevitability of sin, which he interprets as glorifying grace at the expense of free will. (He even goes so far as to equate Augustine's position with B. F. Skinner's contention that there is no personal responsibility for behavior.[23] He calls for the clergy to preach specifically about moral wrongs, lawyers to demand the restructuring of social relationships, the police to merit respect by maintaining high integrity, teachers to model character, the media to exhibit moral concern, statesmen and politicians to act with fidelity to ideals, and doctors—psy-chiatrists in particular—to model a virtuous way of life and counsel about the moral implications of the patient's decisions.

The concerns expressed by Menninger are extended and given a more directly church-related focus in Don S. Browning's *The Moral Context of Pastoral Care*. It is Browning's thesis "that there is a moral context to all acts of care,"[24] and that those profes-sionally responsible for counseling must take that context into account. Like the Hebrew sages of Old Testament times, who counseled in direct relationship to moral obligations enunciated in the Torah, contemporary Christian counselors should be di-rective in dealing with the moral implications of behavior in light of the norms identified with "the Judeo-Christian conglomerate." Too many pastoral counselors have, in contrast, merely bor-rowed psycho-analytical techniques, with their amoral outlook and penchant for adjustment. "On the whole, recent theory and practice of pastoral care has been without an ecclesiology, without an interpretation of modern cultural and institutional life, and without a social ethics."[25]

The upshot of this abandonment of deliberate moral guidance has been to capitulate to the value norms of the civic order, and to add to the moral anomie of the average American middle-class churchgoer. To include the moral dimension in counseling does not mean to dictate decisions, but rather to cultivate a deliberate sense of moral obligation—even a sense of obligation that goes beyond the requirements of the law. Tracing the story of the Christian cure of souls through the early Christian movement, the medieval church and the Protestant Reformation, Browning shows how the moral element functioned in each and how in contrast "pastoral care in twentieth-century mainline Protestant churches has been vastly different from anything seen before in Jewish and Christian history."[26]

Browning develops a model of pastoral care consistent with the premise that moral guidance is a crucial ingredient in the enterprise. The context of moral concern for which Browning pleads is no merely private counseling one, but involves the whole life of the church in the moral nurture of its members.

> The task of religion is to construct a world. The task of the church is to construct an *ethical* world, a world in which forgiveness and renewal simultaneously are possibilities. But what would these two ideas mean in the context of modern societies of rapid social change? It means that the church, in an effort to perform both its general religious task and the task special to its own historical tradition, must create, maintain, modify, and re-create the value symbols of its ethical vision. The church must involve symbols themselves in a rhythm of creation, maintenance, and revision. This is the only way that a truly ethical religiocultural world can be successfully developed. If the church only maintains past moral worlds, it becomes authoritarian and no longer performs realistic and free ethical action designed to combat evil. If it only creates, if it casts its lot with novelty and ceaseless revision, it is simply yielding to the pressures of the moment without testing the efficacy of its own time-proven moral visions and moral rules.[27]

The task of pastoral care as moral inquiry must be related dialectically to the task of pastoral counseling. Pastoral theology must become closely related to theological ethics. "Practical theology goes beyond a theology of pastoral acts and sets forth a theology of practical living—a theology of work, business, marriage, sexuality, child-rearing, aging, youth, etc. Practical theology in this sense of the word is the most neglected of any of the specialties of theology."[28] Browning's agenda does not mean the intensification of punitive sanctions for those who fall away from the expectations of the church as much as it means nurturing persons in the church freely and joyously to embrace the moral vision of Christianity while living in a culture that has all but forgotten it. This involves methodical discipline in religious living—a discipline being sought in odd places by many church members because they do not find it in the churches. Browning argues for the re-creation of a practical moral rationality akin to that practiced in ancient Judaism and in the fidelity to covenant law embraced by the Pharisees.

> We cannot be Christian without first being Jews, or more accurately, without knowing the method of the Jew. We cannot understand the meaning of forgiveness unless we first throw ourselves into a radical concern about the nature of right moral action. We cannot be delivered from the curse of the law unless first of all we know, contemplate, and strive to keep the law.[29]

In a small book written primarily for general use in the church, Thomas C. Oden has added his voice to those who plead for a rediscovery of urgent conscience. He attacks cheap views of freedom from guilt that too easily accept the view that we suffer more from maladjustment than from malfeasance. He pleads for the rigorous conscience that knows guilt to be the real and valid consequence of moral failure, and he extols the power of the Gospel to overcome the legitimate sense of guilt we all experience when breaking the law or defaulting on an obligation. Emphasizing the differences between Christianity and those outlooks that regard moral obligations as repressive, Oden puts the contrasts sharply:

> The heart of the difference between cheap-grace doctrines of guilt-free existence and the Christian gospel is this: Modern chauvinsim desperately avoids the message of guilt by treating it as a regrettable symptom. Christianity intently listens to the message of guilt by conscientious self-examination. Hedonism winks at sin. Christianity earnestly confesses sin. Secularism assumes it can extricate itself from gross misdeeds. Christianity looks to grace for divine forgiveness. Modern consciousness is its own fumbling attorney before the bar of conscience. Christianity rejoices that God himself has become our attorney. Modernity sees no reason to atone for or make reparation for wrongs. Christianity knows that unatoned sin brings on misery of conscience. Modern naturalism sees no need for God. Christianity celebrates God's willingness to suffer for our sins and redeem us from guilt.[30]

The issue posed by those who would stress the importance of acknowledged obligation and the role of the attuned conscience in fostering moral fidelity cannot be collapsed into the debate between advocates of norms and advocates of contexts. While a prescriptive way of defining norms is sometimes associated with an emphasis on moral obligation, it is equally possible to have a very heightened sense of moral responsibility while thinking of norms in deliberative or relational ways. We need to explore the dynamics of moral choice and the conditions under which it develops and is exercised.

9

Moral Development and Moral Choice

Our attention is still on the moral agent and the dynamics of the moral decision, but the focus now shifts from the character or conscience of the agent to the factors that affect the agent in the process of making decisions. Just as conscience has both inner and outer dimensions, so these factors can be said to have both inner and outer aspects. In the material that follows, words like virtue and conscience are eschewed in favor of terms that describe the psychic conditions that either reinforce or block moral responses, terms that indicate processes of moral growth and development, or phenomenological descriptions of the moral choice.

In *The Immobilized Christian: A Study of His Pre-ethical Situation*, John R. Fry contends that debates about norms, or about the relative importance of norms versus contexts, overlook the fact that the private individual has little connection with, or interest in, the ruminations of professional ethicists. Fry, taking note of theoretical issues dividing a theorist of principles like Paul Ramsey from a contextualist like Joseph Sittler, argues that a more fruitful line of reasoning would inquire concerning the

127

pre-ethical situation that determines how the average person (even the average Christian) in fact makes decisions.

The pre-ethical situation involves a private, interior, world about which gestures from one person to another are at best forms of limited communication. "Even though we know from the inside that we are potentially and actually deceptive in whatever re-presentations we make of our interior contents, and even though we know from the inside that whatever re-presentations we receive from other individuals are potentially and actually deceptive, so that we set a veritable filter to trap out distortion, deception, lies, et cetera, this in no way hinders the gesturing that is always going on."[1] To learn from this gesturing, Fry turns to the phenomenologists for instruction, and he suggests that we can get to the contents of the interior life in a preliminary way less by elaborate theory than by the imaginative appropriation of insights. This appropriation can be aided by the reading of some literary fiction, but more particularly by taking our own interior standing ground into account, watching for what is there, and sensing the gestures that others give about what is in their interior world.

Fry proceeds with this "in-standing" through chapters that explore, in turn, how the elementary appetitive drives (such as thirst and hunger) influence our behavior; how erotic factors operate—or, more precisely, are stimulated by our culture to operate—in ways that deeply shape the dimensions of privacy; and how the valuing that each individual does proceeds more according to power, status, or victory in debate than according to rational, helpful, or creative considerations. Fry cites a number of vignettes, which show how an internalized conception of what is legitimate runs counter to, or certainly independent of, legal requirements and moral obligations. "If, as classical moral theory, and classical Christian ethics contends, justice is a norm, that norm is located in the Privacy within a complex framework, almost subscendently, and certainly not transcendently. It may operate transcendently, but it assuredly is located in a real subscendence."[2] Christian ethics should turn its attention to this concrete situation which provides clues to how, indeed, people arrive at their decisions. Paul Lehmann's contextualism, which assumes that Christians take their moral clues from the *koinonia* is wide of the mark because it assumes a functional significance of the church in the life of Christians that simply is not present.

Fry's provocative diagnosis does not deal at any length with the ways in which we can move from the pre-ethical to the ethical situation. "Just what reoriented Christian ethics will do had best not be predicted—only hoped for,"[3] he concludes, pleading for a reorientation toward phenomenal richness.

Moral Nexus: Ethics of Christian Identity and Community by James B. Nelson will seem to some to advance the discussion and to others to fall into the same abstraction Fry decries. There is no mention of Fry in Nelson's book but some of the matters discussed are related. Nelson deliberately minimizes the use of the term conscience because he feels that concepts of selfhood and identity are more useful in making links between ethical reflection and the data given by the social sciences about the ways moral decisions are made. This approach examines "the Christian's moral identity, the pattern and style of his ethics, and the nature of the Christian church in which he participates."[4]

Nelson argues that Christian ethics, both as done on the continent of Europe and in America, has neglected to examine the moral self and the communities in which it lives. Not only must Christian ethics concern itself with the moral agent (as do ethics of virtue and conscience) but it must look at the social factors that influence the decision-making of individuals in behavioral terms. His discussion moves between theological ethics and social psychology (particularly socialization theory, the psychology of moral development, reference group theory, role theory, and identity theory). The book is arranged so that sections on ethical theory alternate with sections giving perspectives from social psychology and sociology.

In part one of his book Nelson argues that ethicists who work from a relational or contextual perspective have done the most to focus attention on the moral self and the importance of the community for the development of that self. In the second part of the book he looks more specifically at insights furnished by social psychology. He examines the importance of the social environment for the development of the moral self—a truly interactional importance. "Not simply a medium through which external forces produce certain results, the self is always involved in the process of interpreting and responding in the light of its interpretations."[5] Noting that socialization involves affective as well as cognitive dimensions, he cites the importance Erikson places on the experience of trust the child gains from parents, how autonomy develops, the onset of initiative, and the movement into adolescence. Nelson then examines the pattern of moral development identified by Jean Piaget, which he feels puts more stress on cognitive elements than Erickson's, and argues that we need both.

Nelson thinks of the stages identified by moral development theory as more suggestive than definitive. He does not feel they are rigidly marked out, nor that movement from one to the next is fixed in order or final in consequence. Persons can go back and forth between stages and it is always possible to regress. Although the stages are structurally similar in different cultures, as Lawrence Kohlberg has demonstrated, they are interactional in every instance. Primary and secondary relationships are crucial for the individual, though different individuals experience these relationships in different ways and with reference to different aspects of the social structure that surrounds them.

Examining the function of roles, Nelson believes it is important to see both how such roles function in relation to shaping values, and how individuals can alter role expectations as well as play them routinely. Looking at identity (the way we see ourselves in relation to others) Nelson shows the essentially social and interactional character of identity and its consequences for our moral decision-making. Reflecting ethically on these matters in part three, Nelson suggests how the components of personal moral ability are engendered and affected by the communities in which we have a part and examines the role played by the church in shaping the decision-making of the selves that belong to it. In contrast to the overwhelming role played by privacy in the argument of Fry, Nelson stresses the importance and reality of social groups, and particularly the capacity of the church to embody more inclusive responses.

In a fourth part of the book, written from the sociological perspective, Nelson turns cultural diagnostician—examining the rise of technology, the advent of the bureaucratic style, and the development of role uncertainty in a changing and pluralistic culture. These developments affect the life of the church as well as life in other structures, and do tend to foreclose the roles the church plays. Such foreclosures are more apparent, Nelson argues, in sect type forms of Christianity than in church types.

In concluding ethical reflections, Nelson develops suggestions for extending the function of the church as a reference group, for utilizing institutional Christianity for the development of moral norms, and for dealing with the church's role as a community of disciples that is simultaneously dutiful and prophetic. Agreeing with T. S. Eliot, whom he quotes, he summarizes his argument by asserting that in order to have life we must live with others, that to live with others we must share in an experience of community, and that to have community we must praise God together. Those experiences are possible only in the church, when it is functioning as a moral community.

One of the most succinct efforts to relate the insights of moral development to religious faith (including the moral dimensions of religious faith) emerged from conversations that originally took place at a colloquium held at the Texas Medical Center in Houston.[6] In the volume that was prepared to report on these conversations, Jim Fowler (who in more formal writing is James W. Fowler) examines theories of moral development in relation to growth in religious faith. Sam Keen, his partner in dialogue, who turns out to be more of the interlocutor than the advocate of an alternative scheme, provides added insights about faith as trust or confidence.

Fowler is concerned with our perceptions of reality, but also with our growth in value perception. He summarizes Piaget's eras and stages and the six stages suggested by Lawrence Kohlberg for moral development and then offers his own theory of faith development with important moral components. Fowler sees no sharp distinction between cognitive and affective dimensions of development. In this he sides with Erikson and Jung and disagrees with Piaget.[7] Moreover, he holds that the transitions between stages are long, often dislocating, and made with great stress. He thinks of the stages as categories to aid interpretation more than as compartments to pigeon-hole human beings. "The stages are not boxes into which people can be stuffed. Rather, they are models by which certain interrelated patterns of our thinking, valuing, and acting may be better understood."[8]

On the basis of extensive interviews with many subjects Fowler advances his own theory of moral/faith development. It consists of six stages, each having seven dimensions. The six stages are: 1) Intuitive-Projective (generally ages 4 to 7 or 8); 2) Mythic-Literal (ages 6 or 7 to 11 or 12); 3) Synthetic-Conventional (ages 11 or 12 to not earlier than 17 or 18 and sometimes characteristic even of adults); 4) Individualistic-Reflexive (beginning no earlier than 17 to 18 but often much later); 5) Paradoxical-Consolidative (rare before age 30 and coming in mid-life, if at all); and 6) Universalizing, which is achieved only in those who overcome "the usual human obsession with survival, security, and significance [and hence come to realize that such enlarged perspectives] threaten measured standards of righteousness, goodness and prudence."[9]

The seven dimensions or characterizing qualities of each stage are: a) different forms of logic operable in each; b) different ways of giving coherence to reality; c) different patterns of role-taking; d) different loci of authority; e) different shapes to social awareness; f) different forms of moral judgment; and g) different uses of symbols. The resulting framework, which Fowler describes at length and charts, enables him to describe a great variety of behaviors and attitudes.

Of particular interest to us are the forms of moral judgment belonging to each of the six stages (though clearly what Fowler says about other characterizing qualities, like attitudes to authority and shapes of social awareness, are relevant for ethics). In stage one the child's conceptions of good and bad are not yet "moral," since the visible consequences in terms of praise and punishment are more determinative than conceptions of right, duty, and obligation. In stage two, elements of reciprocity or fairness enter in terms that Kohlberg describes as "instrumental hedonism" rather than as conceptualized justice. In stage three the person's judgment is concerned with "the expectations of significant others and maintaining agreement or peace between persons."[10] (If found in adults the third stage may appear in conventional terms and have "law and order dimensions.") In stage four the reference group used to calculate moral responsibility widens, and the capacity to take diversity into account develops, although a tendency to caricature the views of others may mean that they are taken into account only by assimilating them into one's own scheme of things. Stage five moves to principled reasoning and utilizes a "higher law" perspective in which the sense of what justice requires coincides with a will to do justice. In stage six, "loyalty to Being is the fundamental principle of moral reasoning,"[11] and the tension between obligation and inclination is overcome. This stage is therefore attained only in an incarnational manner, and in rare personalities.

One of the issues that is raised by moral development theories is whether or not all individuals must move through each of the stages in the same sequence, and whether moral development provides a kind of uniformity of expectation as to how persons behave. Fowler observes that "Kohlberg's stages provide a modern equivalent for the older types of 'natural law' theories of ethics. Kohlberg claims that the stages of moral reasoning, in their formal or structural characteristics, are, like Piaget's stages, sequential, hierarchical, invariant and universal."[12] James B. Nelson, at whose thinking we have already looked, differs on this point, and Donald E. Miller, to whose thinking we said we would return in this chapter, has some important observations to make that bear upon it. These are contained in Miller's discussion of the relations of conscience to reason and the revisions of Kohlberg's theory he feels are necessary to account for that relationship.

Kohlberg, as Miller interprets him, is unconcerned about the relation of the maturing of our moral reasoning to the development of feelings that we have for others. Miller contends that conscience involves both feelings (such as dispositional intentions and the emotions) and coherence (a rational schema, with reason understood more in poetic than in technical terms). Noting that Piaget and Kohlberg have attempted to resolve the rift between emotivists and intuitionalists by postulating a developmental scheme with invariant sequences, Miller contends that they have separated the technical mode of reason from the poetic and have tended to overlook ways in which socio-emotive factors are bound together with cognitive ones in human agency. Consequently, "Kohlberg's account of right thinking must be supplemented, perhaps modified, by an account of right feeling such as Erikson's."[13] Concern about the growth of "sympathy for humanity" must complement the cognitive elements involved in understanding of moral development. The consistency and dependability of the caring community, which supports and accepts persons non-punitively, is a crucial aspect of development. The reason and the conscience are related at all ages, but the reason functions differently in the child than it does in the adult, and it is just as important to be aware of changes in reasoning that occur during growth as it is to be aware of the changes in valuing. The process of arriving at both moral understanding and religious belief must allow young people to test out both provisionally before becoming permanently committed—and any framework that does not allow for such a process of inquiry truncates the desirable pattern for maturation.

The "postconventional conscience" should go beyond utilitarianism, to a concern for a more just world community, perhaps even to a decision to sacrifice oneself for a cause, to a sense that "emotions, intentions, intuitions and social relationships are just as important as formal thought in an adequate account of the strength of agency."[14] For Miller, a crucial ingredient in moral education is exposure to a variety of life-styles, the appreciation of their similarities and differences, and the cultivation of capacities for overcoming limited and self-justifying loyalties to only one pattern.

Possibly the fullest discussion of moral decision-making and its complex interrelationships with selfhood and social environment published during the period that concerns us is Daniel C. Maguire's *The Moral Choice*. This overview of the subject is prefaced by a diagnosis of conditions that make for moral confusion in modern society—conditions similar but not identical to those discussed by Fry but seen by Maguire as far more social and cultural in quality. Maguire also identifies advocates of four theoretical positions which he feels miss the meaning of morality: the realists, who reduce morality to custom; the survivalists, who make it a matter of maintaining existence without a necessary concern for its quality; the linguistic analysts, who play with language clarification instead of exploring commitments; and the presumers, who deal with a variety of practical issues without explicating the foundational values involved in making decisions about them. As an alternative to these dodges, Maguire defends an "ethical realism," in which the foundations of morality rest on a relationship that benefits persons as persons and upon an experience of sacredness which gives that concern about persons and their environment a special, and yet unprovable, claim on our loyalties. The moral enterprise rests, then, upon belief in the sanctity of life and those responses of affection, faith, and process through which we honor that sanctity, even to the point of risk to our own lives.

Being ethical is not a simple process of arriving at merely intellectual judgments about what is morally required. "Ethics is *the art-science which seeks to bring sensitivity and method to the discernment of moral values.*"[15] It does involve thinking and discernment—partly as a matter of science (discerning an objective reality) and partly as a matter of art (involving skill, taste, and imagination). According to Maguire, effective ethical choice is blocked both by lack of theoretical clarity and by inadequate personality development. Because the two are so closely intertwined his suggestions constitute neither an account of moral reasoning by itself nor merely an analysis of moral agency, but a morphology of moral choice that involves their combination.

Moral decision-making, as Maguire portrays it, centers on a group of questions that pose the issue "How do we know?" These questions begin with the attempt to identify *what* is being considered (or talked about) in the discussion of an ethical issue. Failure to describe accurately the practice or practices being evaluated—and such failures have been and continue to be prevalent and occasionally appalling—simply renders moral discourse either tangential to the real issue or even disconnected from it. Along with the proper identification of the object of moral reflection we also need to ascertain *"why* we are doing something and *how* we are doing it."[16] This opens up issues of motive, intention and purpose. About these, also, moral discourse is woefully inexact, even though it is not possible to have adequate moral inquiry without knowing about them. Style is an important feature of ethics, for it is possible to be correct about issues and honest in their portrayal, yet harsh, insensitive, or inept in handling them. The status of the person or persons involved also shapes the moral decision; since people vary enormously in backgrounds, personal qualities, circumstances, and outlooks, decisions cannot be made without reference to such variations. Likewise, *when* and *where* are variables that must be factored in when judging whether particular actions should or should not be performed. Ethical decisions must also be examined in light of viable alternatives and foreseeable effects—not necessarily because these dictate the action to be taken (as consequentialism holds), but because the implications of decisions are pertinent as well as their value premises. In a complex, technological world "posterity is the neighbor whom we must love as ourselves if the future is to have a chance."[17] To love posterity (even to love the present fellow being) as a neighbor requires that we be as informed as possible about technical factors and the alternative possibilities they create.

Bearing upon the question and issues at the center of moral decisions are eight faculties or skills. Maguire diagrams these as spokes on a wheel whose hub consists of the central questions. These spokes, which describe qualities brought to the decision by the moral agent, include 1) creative imagination; 2) principles that enable consistency in approach to issues but a consistency that does not preclude a capacity to understand exceptions and surprises; 3) the power of rational analysis; 4) a proper respect for the contributions from authority; 5) sensitized affections that guide feelings as to what is, or is not, appropriate; 6) individual experiences; 7) group history as a source of knowledge and understanding about a matter in question; 8) a sense of humor, which enables creative responses to incongruity or surprise, and facilitates joy and delight; and 9) a capacity to cope with tragedy. These various elements are described in a way that involves both normative judgments and agency skills.

Having formed this morphology of moral decision-making (not merely of moral reasoning, though reasoning is involved) Maguire considers the nature of conscience, which he defines as *"the conscious self as attuned to moral values and disvalues in the concrete."*[18] He rejects the view that conscience is an innate faculty which provides direct moral judgments. He acknowledges its conditioned specificities from person to person and the contingent factors in its development that explain why equally conscientious people differ on issues. Conscience consists of the internalized forms of the faculties or skills, which are the spokes of the wheel that diagrams the moral decision.

> Conscience always bears the distinguishing marks of each person's unique moral odyssey. It is historically conditioned and developed. But what each conscience will have in common with all others is its roots in the core of the foundational moral experience. Conscience will always give form to our natural status as social beings. What is innate in all of this is that we are born persons, naturally geared to relate harmoniously and fruitfully with other persons. The shape and activity of our individual conscience is not innate. It is the product of our decisions, our education, our personal formative encounters— in a word, of our history.[19]

Maguire's discussion of the nature of guilt is particularly pertinent when seen against the issues we discussed in the previous chapter. He acknowledges that some guilt can be symptomatic of psychic illness. "There can, of course, be a sick guilt. We can feel the agony of remorse when there is really nothing objective that we should be regretting or feeling responsible for."[20] But, "there is such a thing as healthy guilt—guilt that is not neurotic and that calls not so much for therapy as for moral conversion."[21]

The concluding chapter of *The Moral Choice*, entitled "The Hazards of Moral Discourse," deals with various "filters," which prevent ethics from being complete and final. These include myths, cognitive moods, false analogies, abstractions, selective vision, role, and banalization. This list is not presented as exhaustive, since even reflection about moral choice is not final or perfected. "Ethics can only seek to bring method and some completeness to [the] human conversation on moral values from which no one is dispensed. If it does that even somewhat well, it has served a world which is, thus far, more clever than wise."[22]

The various forms of interest in moral agency that are present in contemporary ethical reflection add much to the considerations given to the formulation of norms and development of strategies to implement ethics. But there are other concerns that require attention, if the account of the current developments is to be comprehensive. One of these is the rise of moral thinking in relationship to vocational problems and policy-decisions.

IV

New Frameworks

10

Ethics in Vocational and Policy-Making Settings

Thinking about the qualities of moral agency has a counterpart in thinking about the frameworks in which ethicists go about their work. By "framework" we mean a special setting within which the process of viewing things and considering value questions takes place or a special agenda that focuses moral attention upon particular issues. In this section we will be looking at three very different, and interestingly contrasting, frameworks that have come to focus the concerns or solicit the attention of Christian ethicists, starting with vocationally oriented ethics and policy-making.

At least since the Reformation, Christian vocation has been understood to involve service of God in the productive and professional activities that sustain daily life, and Christian ethicists have been attentive to the fact that moral questions arise in the course of daily work. But it is only in recent years that the particular forms of daily work have become major frameworks for exploring ethical issues. For example, assessing the state of Christian ethics in 1965, James Gustafson spoke about the "ethical problems of medical care."[1] This rubric implies that normal Christian insights are utilized to deal with a special set of problems. Today, the common terminology is "bio-medical ethics." This signifies a special field of interest to which Christian ethicists may have contributions to make, but which draws its main impetus and categories of thought from the examination of the professional problems of a particular group. The same metamorphosis can be discerned in business ethics, legal ethics, and engineering ethics.

This set of developments interestingly follows a much longer set of changes in our higher educational system in which the ethical aspects of competence in the arts and sciences were given less and less direct attention. As Douglas Sloan has observed, at one period the teaching of moral philosophy occupied a central place in the undergraduate curriculum.

> Throughout most of the nineteenth century, the most important course in the college curriculum was moral philosophy, taught usually by the college president, and required of all senior students. The moral philosophy course was regarded as the capstone of the curriculum. It aimed to pull together, to integrate, and to give meaning and purpose to the student's entire college experience and course of study. In so doing, it even more importantly also sought to equip the graduating seniors with the ethical sensitivity and insight needed if they were to put their newly acquired knowledge to use in ways that would benefit not only themselves and their own personal advancement, but the larger society as well.[2]

Students entering the learned professions from a college background with the focus Sloan describes were not unprepared to cope with ethical issues arising in the course of their work. But, as Sloan indicates, this kind of instruction waned at the turn of the century and was followed for a period of time by a blossoming of interest in professional ethics. The schools training for the learned professions paid increased attention to some of the problems that young lawyers, journalists, and business executives were likely to face, but even this interest was soon to be eclipsed by the same reductionisms that had taken a toll in the undergraduate curriculum.

By 1964, which is approximately the time that begins the period being studied in this survey, the situation for the study of ethics was dismal. Sloan's analysis continues:

A 1964 article presenting a sampling of 100 college and university catalogs—representing institutions of all types, large and small, public and private, religious and secular—found that only 27 institutions "required any philosophy at all for graduation with the bachelor of arts degree." And ethics was only one among several fields within philosophy itself. The author of that study noted that in his own institution of 12,000 students the enrollment in ethics averaged 11 students per year. His institution was probably fairly representative. By the mid-1960s the teaching of ethics was in deep trouble.[3]

Admittedly, as Sloan indicates, there was a close connection in the 1950s and 1960s between the teaching of religion—then expanding in the collegiate setting—and the exploration of ethical issues. But the teaching of religion was under pressures to "adopt the standards of graduate-school oriented professionalism," and this pressure rendered at least some teaching of religion less likely to address ethical matters than it might have been.

We must certainly grant the significance to the situation Sloan describes, for education does have an influence in shaping the public ethos and the capacity of individuals to understand value questions. If it does not exercise that influence it leaves a void that has to be filled whenever problems arise with pressing urgency.

The interest of religion in moral issues during the same period tended to polarize at two ends of a spectrum that left out the vocational concerns. On the one hand much American religion preoccupied itself with a privatized afterlife, and with a narrow conception of moral goodness that had little to say about specific issues arising in the vocational context. On the other hand, and often in reaction to developments toward individualistic moralism, both the Social Gospel and the Social Realism that followed it focused on social and political agendas that were as far removed as the private orientations from the places where many vocational problems are acutely felt by most professionals.

Interest in the ethics of the vocations has arisen since 1967 to an extent that would have been unimaginable at the beginning of the period. The most obvious instance of the growth of such interest is related to the medical profession. One of the factors prompting medical professionals to be interested was their escalating capacity to prolong life without at the same time enhancing its viability. The comatose patient—technically living because of medicine's "success" but doing so at enormous cost to family or society with seemingly no hope of recovery or of meaningful existence—poses hard questions about the very achievements of medicine itself. Unprecedented choices developed, some of them (like allocating scarce resources under conditions that make a difference between life and death) having excruciating implications. Since bio-ethics began, medical advances have taken place at a staggering pace, and many new dilemmas have arisen, particularly from genetic manipulation and other techniques for making fundamental alterations to the human species. Even the legitimacy of research itself has come into question.

These problems were felt acutely by doctors, and conversations with ethicists came readily. The ethicists were learning about the problems even as the doctors were facing them. Bio-medical ethics (or bio-ethics) was born from this felt need, and grew because resources were found to bring doctors and ethicists (mainly theological ethicists) together in centers for the exploration of issues. The work accomplished has been enormous—though medical advances seem to have posed issues at least as fast as ethical reflection can provide insights regarding the appropriate uses of the known techniques. The interdisciplinary factor is crucial, for in most instances the necessary understanding of technical factors is possessed mainly by the health professional, and the ethicist only faces the issues as they are interpreted to him. "As a result, the questions and problems of bioethics come much easier and faster than resolutions—or even clear statements—of the problems."[4]

The literature that has appeared from this undertaking is already vast, and growing at an escalating rate. It takes regular bibliographical attention even to list the forthcoming materials.[5] Many theological ethicists have made individual contributions to this growing literature, though relatively few of the books were written before the mid-1960s.[6]

Initially, the preoccupations of bio-medical ethics were the problems that arise in curative therapy. These are the problems directly felt by the doctor in "the crisis atmosphere of the intensive care unit, the pathos of the intensive care nursery, and the specter of practically incomprehensible developments and application of new research techniques. . ."[7] The problems that subsequently arose from scientific research and engineering—genetic engineering, in vitro fertilization, and the use of human beings for experimentation—have made the "bio" part of the term as important as the "medical". Bio-medical ethics has not been as ready to deal with the social policy matters surrounding the practice of medicine, or with the problems that arise in interprofessional relationships within the medical enterprise. Until recently there has been little discussion of the financing of medical services as an ethical problem, about policy matters related to the availability of medical education to all segments of the society, about the equal distribution of competent care to areas of the country having unequal attractiveness as places to practice, or about the problems involved in the self-policing of the technical competency of the profession.[8]

Business ethics is possibly as extensive as bio-medical ethics but the direct involvement of Christian ethicists has not been as central. The ethical problems raised by economic processes and the conduct of business affairs have been canvassed at workshops and conferences for many years, and a considerable literature has been produced under the rubric of business ethics.[9] New material is constantly emerging, though the contributions of theological ethicists continue to be far less evident in this field than in the case of bio-ethics.[10]

Donald G. Jones identifies three concerns under the heading of business ethics. "The first level could be called *Macro-Ethics of a Market Economy*, the second level, *Business and Social Policy*, and the third, *Management* ethics."[11] The issues and materials associated with the first level would be similar to those that were once considered under rubrics such as "Christianity and Economic Problems." In his book *The Radical Imperative*,[12] John C. Bennett re-emphasizes the importance of these issues and reaffirms some of the approaches he took toward them early in his career. The rise of the multinational corporation makes the matters to be dealt with on the first level increasingly global in scope, and Christian theologians join with others in addressing them.

The second level identified by Jones emphasizes more directly the role and function of the corporation and the effects of its practices on society. The third level examines the problems associated with the exercise of the managerial function and from one perspective could alone be said to represent the doing of ethics in the vocational context. Considerations belonging to both the second and third level underscore the many dimensions of institutionalism as a motif in Christian ethics. Much institutionalism is concerned with political structures, and thinking about it tends to gravitate in that direction too easily. Many social organizations have bureaucratic rather than political dimensions. Max Weber saw the growing importance of bureaucracy and its incipient threats to individual liberty and personal creativity, but he did not think that the threat comes from governmental bureaucracies alone. He perceived the dehumanizing impact of modern industrialized capitalism, but unlike Marx (who felt the dangers were in the maldistribution of property) Weber felt them to come from the poor utilization and management of all bureaucracies, those of the private sector as well as those of the state. The preoccupation with efficiency and the drive to rationalize all productive processes by its tests produces "an iron cage of serfdom"[13] in both capitalistic and socialistic economies.

Business ethicists have been aware of these matters for some time. For example, in 1959, Benjamin M. Selekman, a Harvard Business School professor with acknowledged roots in the Hebrew Christian tradition, judged that the amoral rationality Weber deemed inevitable was fading away in favor of a moral/ evaluational set of concerns.

> So the search for a moral philosophy continues. Behind this search are two primary causes: the hostility directed against business beginning with the Great Depression of the thirties and the growth of a new professional management class, as distinguished from the owner-manager of former days, who

built his own business, was the principal stockholder, and ran it either by himself or with those whom he took in as partners. Recent decades have witnessed a veritable explosion in business education, with large enrollments in business schools affiliated with universities. Association with a university immediately projects any calling on a technical and moral plane, with the challenge to meet standards already established in the older professions of law, medicine, engineering, architecture, the ministry, and teaching. With the concept of a profession comes also a self-consciousness, a desire to develop standards of technical performance as well as an ethical code, both of which give dignity and stature to those who enter the calling."[14]

If the analysis that Douglas Sloan has made of the demise of moral concern in higher education is correct, then some of the contributions which Selekman felt would accrue from relating business more closely to the university were sliding away at the very time he was hoping to benefit from them. The concern shown by Selekman does show that business ethics is not entirely new in its conceptualization, though the degree of attention shown to it may be much increased since Selekman wrote and the intensity of the issues greatly magnified. It is in the latter sense that Charles Powers and David Vogel are correct in identifying an increased interest in business ethics as having four causes: (1) concern about the growing size of institutions of all types and about their impact upon individual lives and political processes; (2) a growth in the legal restraints on business and the involvement of government in decisions and activities that affect business affairs; (3) public concern about the external consequences of large corporate organizations that are not amenable to direct market control; and (4) an increase in the priority attached to human dignity by the society at large.[15]

The situation with respect to legal ethics is quite complex. On the one hand, it is impossible to understand the law as either a norm-setting or an adjudicating process without having to deal with issues having central significance in ethics. As Harold Berman has shown, there are many similarities both between law and religion and between legal and religious institutions.[16] On the other hand, the advocacy system makes the lawyer responsible to represent the interests of the client irrespective of the client's guilt or innocence in a crime, and in civil litigation it legitimizes advocacy without a necessary obligation to approve of the claim at bar. Idealistic students sometimes feel compunctions about assuming the advocacy role in some circumstances, particularly if they are less than fully sure about the capacity of the larger system to adjudicate claims in a morally and socially responsible manner.

The legal profession has been debating its ethic in connection with the adoption of a proposed new code of professional responsibility. One of the more controversial matters has been the specification of the lawyer's obligation to provide professional services to those who cannot afford the usual fees. The long-standing code says only "Every lawyer shall support all proper efforts to meet this need." A proposed requirement that suggested a system of obligatory *pro bono* work—forty hours per year—was dropped in favor of a self-reporting system to encourage individual efforts,[17] but even the more lenient requirement aroused opposition. This debate illustrates the tension that develops between thinking of vocational ethics as indicating ideals for individuals to follow and a more socially oriented perspective.

The present code envisions the lawyer almost entirely in the role of an advocate for a clearly identified client who pays for the services, with a similar lawyer for the client on the other side. It requires the lawyer to "represent the client zealously within the bounds of the law" and to keep the client's secrets inviolable. The proposed revision thinks of the lawyer more as a statesperson of the legal system and a guardian of the public interest that hangs upon the proper function of that system. Under the long-standing code the lawyer cannot disclose a client's confidences; the revision would allow such disclosure to prevent a client from committing an act that would result in death or serious harm. The debate about which outlook should govern is a legitimate one—since the premise of confidence is crucial for the candor upon which the client relationship is established, but the protection of life is an equally weighty matter, even as judged by the client's interest. The fact that the matter is being debated is indicative of one tension that is at the heart of legal ethics.

It is not easy to delineate the exact scope of the interest in the relationship of religion to law. Lynn Robert Buzzard has prepared an annotated bibliography, *Law and Theology*.[18] It covers an extensive body of material, including general works on jurisprudence (the relation of law to natural law, to morality, and to justice); treatments of the interface between law and religion (mainly Christianity and law, and the Bible and law); discussions of the professional life of the lawyer; and specific issues (such as church and state, civil disobedience, crime and punishment). Some book-length treatments of legal ethics from a general philosophical perspective are found in this listing, but very few are written specifically from a theological perspective.[19] Nothing has yet emerged as extensive as those treatments that have covered issues in the bio-medical field from the perspective of theological ethics.

The relationship of Christianity and the practice of law has been the focal interest of the Christian Legal Society, an association of lawyers, law students, and judges, founded in 1961 and concerned with the relationship of law and its practice to a confessionally defined Christianity. In 1975 this society founded a Center for Law and Religious Freedom for the defense of those whose rights as Christians to exercise and express their faith are being infringed. The Society publishes a quarterly journal, a periodical news-letter, and other materials dealing with issues germane to its agenda.

The relationship of religious faith and the understanding and practice of law has also been addressed by a group called the Committee on Religion and Law (CORAL). This group, which includes lawyers, law students, theologians, and ethicists from a variety of religious backgrounds, also publishes a news-letter. It has sponsored consultations and conferences which have explored the relationship of religion and law as well as the ethical issues arising from the practice of the legal vocation. In addition to CORAL, there has been a special group within the Society of Christian Ethics that has focused attention on the ethical aspects of law and the practice of law. Many members of the SCE group are also members of CORAL.

James F. Bresnahan, writing in the *Journal of Legal Education* in 1976, took note of the strong pressures for teaching ethics to law students that arose in the Watergate period and declared

> . . . if ethical issues of legal practice are to be treated in a thorough, intellectually challenging, straightforward and effective way, not only in the formation of law students but also in the on-going preservation and enhancement of professional competence of practitioners, the legal profession must tighten the active bonds between the practicing bar and the teaching bar, and together they must obtain the technical advice of persons specializing in ethics.[20]

Bresnahan is not as clear in his assessment of legal ethics as Jones is in his assessment of business ethics about the limited input on these matters coming from Christian ethicists, but he would certainly agree with Michael J. Kelly that "there is a profound gap between the materials available either for an ethics course or courses in other subjects that raise ethical issues, and the world of decision-making by attorneys."[21]

Engineering education is increasingly concerned with the impact of technology upon both the society and the environment. Such a concern is closely related to, but may be pursued independently of, questions about appropriate values in the professional practice of engineering. "The field of engineering ethics must be distinguished clearly from the related but quite different field of the study of the ethical (and other) impacts of technology. The latter field is concerned primarily with the study of the objects and organized systems of objects which fall under the general description, 'technological.' In contrast, the field of engineering ethics is concerned with the actions and decisions made by persons, individually or collectively, who belong to the profession of engineering."[22]

This distinction by Professor Robert J. Baum must be kept in mind, but concerns in both areas are present in engineering education and bear upon the ethical training of persons in the sciences and technology. Indeed, one of the major program emphases of the World Council of Churches in the period covered by this survey has been with Science, Technology, and the Future, and it has brought scientists and theologians into conversations with each other.[23] Moreover, subjects such as technology assessment—the art of trying to measure beforehand the social and environmental consequences of a new technology, and technology transfer—the study of the consequences of the movement of technology from one nation to another, are new and important ways of referring to issues related to a vocational context even if they are of broader concern to a general public.

The extent to which the contributions of theological ethicists have been welcomed in programs dealing with science and society or with the vocational problems of scientists and engineers has varied greatly. Some large and distinguished centers of scientific learning are open to the contributions of theologians and even deliberately seek it for programs in Science, Theology, and Human Values. Others are oblivious or even hostile to the possible contributions of theologically informed analysis and inquiry. There seems to be no easy explanation of the variations in terms of identifiable factors such as public versus private, large versus small, renowned versus marginal, types of institution.

There has been relatively little work done with respect to the two learned vocations most immediately related to the usual Christian ethicist.[24] Practically no attention has been given to the ethical problems arising from the practice of ministry, though the role of the church with respect to social issues has been hotly debated.[25] Similarly, Christian ethicists have produced relatively few sustained treatments of the ethical problems that arise in teaching as a vocation or in the governance of academic institutions. To be sure, among faculties there is much shoptalk, frequent complaining about the inadequacy of administrators, and considerable expenditure of energy on the protection of prerogatives, but not much probing into the exercise of the pedagogical function, or into the moral questions raised by the pursuit of knowledge, e.g., about the individualistic structure of a reward system, or the temptations of a largely self-regulated schedule. Perhaps these questions will be addressed more fully in the future. Much will depend upon the extent to which academicians become curious and candid about things that impinge most closely upon their own activities, and also upon the extent to which the examination of these questions becomes the object of private and public funding.

Each of the areas of vocationally related ethics raises issues, not only about the conduct of individuals engaged in a given practice but about public policy. Inquiry into the making of public policy has become a special way of thinking, sometimes centered in colleges or universities and sometimes in new centers or institutes especially devised for the purpose. The growth of such institutes has been one of the emerging phenomena of recent years.

When moral philosophy was dominant in nineteenth-century higher education, the cultural situation was simpler and consensus about values was more apparent—at least in ideological terms. Moral philosophy confirmed the individual's moral striving and at the same time served the needs of culture by articulating values generally shared in the civic order. Many theologians at this time strongly argued, following Scottish common sense philosophy, that it was possible to achieve the same certainty and exactness with moral knowledge as was then trumpeted to be possible in knowing the laws of nature. Sabbath observance, for instance, was warranted as mandatory for both individuals and society with an argument about its functional necessity for human life.

The task of policy-making in today's society is much more complex, not least because the value-pluralism of our society is much greater, is often cherished as itself of value,[26] and in any event contributes to a situation in which the study of ethics as the enunciation of a set of universally shared agreements is impossible. While many yearn for the recrudescence of a unified cultural ethos, and advance proposals for putting the power of the state behind the legal enforcement of particular moral judgments which they hold (and hold that all others should likewise hold), the unanimity upon which such programs need to be based eludes us. Any effort to create it by fiat has all the incipient dangers of past noble experiments or of clerically based fundamentalism. What college president today, except in an institution self-defined confessionally, would dare to offer the graduating seniors a course on moral philosophy as a consensus guide to individual and public practice?

On the other hand, pluralism rampant can mean public life chaotic. If all judgments are up for grabs, if no course of action is wiser than any other, if the final operative measure of social acceptability is who can get away with what, with how much, how fast, and with how little cost, we are in danger as a society. If politics is merely the process of obtaining power by any means—or, at least by almost any means—or if it is merely the process of determining who is going to rule rather than for what ends, our society will be quite different from one in which a set of shared values, however minimally identified, helps to give it cohesion and to influence decision-making.

Policy studies stand midway between ethics as a search for definitions of the right, the good, or the fitting, and politics in the sense of settling who will have control. At the heart of policy analysis is a concern for which values and purposes are to be served by what means of control. To use an overly simplified illustration, while ethics is concerned with judging stealing to be wrong, policy studies would be concerned to ask by what means it is possible to curtail it without at the same time doing harm to other values in the society (such as civil liberty). Policy is concerned with the moral evaluation of strategy, not merely with the evaluation of its effectiveness. It has always been an ingredient in social ethics and in politics. What may be new is the effort to give it independent standing and to pursue it as a mode of analysis to be done in special settings.

Another way to think about policy studies—or the policy sciences, as they are sometimes called—is to conceive of them as an effort to do the evaluating often associated with ethics, or with religion, in a manner characteristic of the sciences. Evaluating is often accompanied by argument and controversy; scientific procedures are felt to rely upon a mastery of data and the examination of alternatives. Policy studies hope to achieve the consequences of moral reflection, attended by the credibility enjoyed by science.

All that goes by the magic name is not the authentic reality. Many of the groups which have utilized the term in their self-description are faithful to the canons of inquiry—but some are not. The examination of policy questions needs to be free from ideological prior-restraint. The openness of inquiry cherished in the college or university context is an important way to provide the yearned-for credibility. It is all too easy to set up a policy research organization with so heavy a commitment to a predisposed agenda as to create suspicion almost from the start. Conversely, it is impossible to engage in the evaluation of strategy from a totally neutral perch. As long as policy studies examine agendas and strategies evaluatively they share the risks of moral reflection in a pluralistic ethos. But qualities of intellectual fairness, of the determination to understand the positions of others accurately and without caricature, and to canvass alternatives before making conclusions—these are qualities one hopes to find in the academic world and which should come to the fore in policy studies as well. To the extent they do, policy studies will call forth the best in critical thinking even though they will not transform choice-making into an objective science.

The changes in ethics that have been brought about by giving attention to the vocational and policy-making framework are important. They include inter-disciplinary achievements resulting from face-to-face explorations between Christian ethicists and persons at work in other fields. Many Christian ethicists have come to deal with questions of value and problems of strategy without first achieving prior agreement about theological categories or doctrinal matters. A new vocabulary has emerged, designed to communicate with persons of many skills and diverse commitments. A number of theological ethicists have studied in, and even joined faculties of, professional schools of medicine, law and engineering.

The middle ground between purely personal morality and an almost wholly official or public approach has been discovered and explored. This has even occurred with respect to considering the ethics of public life, where the distinction between the policy-making role of some and the civil-servant role of others, as drawn very sharply by Max Weber in *Politics as a Vocation*, has been challenged.[27]

The use of the case study method has been advanced in teaching of ethics in all fields. The importance of casuistical approaches has been emphasized.

Finally, new institutional settings, financed in new ways, have been created and opportunities developed for teaching and thinking about ethics in quite different settings. A new body of literature has emerged quite different in focus and approach from that previously available. But even with all this, many persons equally concerned with Christian ethics have been uninvolved in these trends. The next chapter will discuss one group about which this is the case.

11

Liberation Theology
as a Source of Ethics

The term liberation has a long history of theological meaning, but the extent to, and forcefulness with, which it has recently been employed provides a framework for ethics that places emphases in new areas and makes distinctive claims for new concerns.

Nor is it an inconsequential accident that the term liberation has been used to designate, not a particular kind of ethic, but rather a particular approach to an entire theological enterprise. Each of the movements of diverse origin and rigorous vitality that designates itself as a form of liberation theology has a strong social ethics agenda, and each emphasizes the importance of making freedom something to be sought, not merely thought about. The starting point for liberation theologies is "from below"—from a view of the world shared by the disinherited who suffer under, rather than worry about the proper use of, established institutions and instruments of political power.

No social ethic can altogether ignore any one of the three factors of freedom, order, and power—but the priority that is attached to these makes an enormous difference in how society is understood, where emphases are placed, and how strategies are developed to deal with social matters. Much institutionalism gives priority to order (since order is understood as ensuring freedom and legitimizing power); much operationalism gives priority to power (because it believes that power shapes policy and even guards liberty). Liberation theologies give priority to freedom, and they define freedom as having three dimensions: (1) the aspiration of the oppressed for liberation from the control of their destiny by others; (2) the aspiration of persons to control their own history; and (3) overcoming of the power of sin by a power appropriated and shared with Christ. Freedom thus comes to be the overarching category under which justice, selfhood, and salvation are subsumed. As Letty Russell puts it, quoting in the process Jürgen Moltmann (the European political theologian of hope) and Rubem Alves (the South American theologian of futurism):

> The horizon of freedom is hope! Hope is the expectation of faith that God's promised future will become a reality. . . .
> The situation of variability of liberation leads to a constant shifting of our horizon of freedom. We might hope for liberation as freedom from outside coercion and causation, or for a spontaneous affirmation of selfhood. At another time our hope might be for freedom as an alternative possibility for change or for freedom of choice and freedom to act on that choice. Yet our human hopes as Christians are always based on the perfect freedom of God. It is God's perfect freedom which is exercised in *being for us*. According to Moltmann, "God is not our utopia, but we are God's utopia. We are hoping because God hopes for us." . . . Rubem Alves describes the horizon of freedom in saying: "The cross, then, which is fundamentally the symbol of the hopelessness and futurelessness that order and religion created, came to be seen as the beginning of a new possibility for history. . . . Because . . . [God] suffers with and negates the unfreedom of today, it is possible to hope for a tomorrow in which . . . [we] will be made free."[1]

Similarly, James Cone, writing about the priority and centrality of freedom, has observed:

> Freedom is that structure of and movement in human existence which enables people to struggle against slavery and oppression. History is the place in which freedom actualizes itself;

and hope is the anticipation of freedom that is actualized in history. Hope is freedom's vision, and history is the context in which the vision takes shape. Freedom, history, and hope are bound together, expressing humanity's constitution, its place and also its future realization. When freedom is separated from history, it is no longer authentic freedom. It is an opium, a sedative which makes people content with freedom's opposite, oppression. Freedom is also denied when it is separated from hope, the vision of a new heaven and new earth. Hope is freedom's transcendence, the soul's recognition that "what *is* ain't supposed to be." History is freedom's immanence, the recognition that what *is* is the place where we have been called to bear witness to the future, the "not yet" of human existence. Freedom then is a project, not an object. It is the projection of self in history against the structures of oppression in order to bear witness to the coming realm of perfect freedom.[2]

Liberation theologies extend themes present in both the theology of hope and political theology. They call into question both the privileged standing of Christians and Christian institutions in Western culture and the intellectual adequacy of theological reflection built upon dominant Western models. Their self-designation as theologies rather than as ethical systems means that they are concerned with the change of an entire world-view rather than with the formulation of different norms within an existing framework or with the recasting of strategy within a continuing social matrix. Robert McAfee Brown's description of liberation theologies as *Theology in a New Key* underscores the extent to which a new framework has developed—one that makes a common demand to be freed from oppression and to be heard and heeded in asserting the necessity of social change. Brown holds that dominant theologies are able to muster only reformist impulses, if indeed even those, and therefore do not provide the "fulcrums of change for the creation of a social order that embodies justice for all rather than privilege for a few."[3]

Each theology of liberation has distinctive features, a special setting, and an understandable yearning. But the common elements are the position at the bottom of the ladder of inequality in the society to which each is relegated and a perception of reality from that vantage point. The "view from below" which differentiates liberation from dominant theologies has, according to Brown, six characteristics:[4]

1. A different starting point: Instead of the empirical examination of nature, turning to traditional authority to vindicate truths, or engagement in rational inquiry as a source of judgment, liberation theologies start with the experience of being marginalized or excluded.

2. A different interlocutor: Instead of the non-believer with intellectual difficulties about the viability of religious faith, the interlocutor to whom liberation theologies listen is the person (really a "non-person") who has been crushed by or excluded from the surrounding social situation.

3. A different set of tools: Instead of philosophy, which uses the tools of metaphysical speculation and linguistic analysis, liberation theologians use the insights of sociologists and political thinkers (often of Marxists) to inquire concerning reality and to form concepts for describing and understanding it.

4. A different analysis: Instead of assuming that harmony is a normal condition between peoples and neutrality a clue to being fair and equitable, liberation theology regards conflict as a given corollary of injustice and looks upon identification with the oppressed in the struggle against injustice as the necessary way to overcome ideological blindness.

5. A different mode of engagement: Instead of searching for a theory the truth of which is settled as a first premise and then its implications drawn out, liberation theology works out truth and theory in continual interrelationship with action and involvement. This is known as *praxis*.

6. A different theology: Instead of seeking understandings drawn from perceptions of "the God above" (transcendent) and imposed on the world, theology becomes critical reflection on *praxis*, and develops from what we learn and experience by seeking to transform the world as Christians work (alongside of God) on behalf of the poor.

The locating of freedom in the autonomy of the political sphere rather than in the autonomy of the rational self has momentous consequences for the handling of ethical concepts.

The Kantian formulations, marked by universalizable rules and categorical imperatives, are superseded by tests of legitimacy involving identification with the purposes of a particular group. The meaning of universality is no longer related to rational formulations which all thinking persons can accept, but to the fact "that all oppressed peoples become [Christ's] people."[5] The categorical imperative comes to be defined, not in terms of a general principle that is understood and applied alike by all, but in terms of a specific thrust that is felt and followed only as the oppressed attain their freedom from bondage.

In his book *A Black Theology of Liberation*, James H. Cone forcefully portrays Black Theology as a theology which arises from the experience of an oppressed community. "Unlike white theology which tends to make the Christ-event an abstract, intellectual idea, Black Theology believes that the black community itself is precisely where Christ is at work. The Christ-event in twentieth century America is a black-event, that is, an event of liberation taking place in the black community in which black people recognize that it is incumbent upon them to throw off the chains of white oppression by whatever means they regard as suitable."[6] Cone charges that white American theology from Puritans to the death-of-God theologians has served white interests and rationalized the oppression of blacks. Therefore white theology is doomed. Its search for general principles—its belief that what is universalizable must be above distinctions between groups—has no cogency for those it victimizes. "The revolutionary situation forces Black Theology to shun all abstract principles dealing with what is the 'right' and 'wrong' course of action. There is only one principle which guides the thinking and action of Black Theology: an unqualified commitment to the black community as that community seeks to define its existence in light of God's liberating work in the world."[7] Black Theology understands struggle—struggle against genocide, struggle against the effort to destroy ethnic identity, struggle against the insanity of white racism. It rejects all appeals to Providence that counsel submission, that urge acceptance of limits, that speak abstractly or dispassionately when passion is demanded. The sources of

Black Theology are in black history, black experience, and black culture; revelation and tradition cannot be rightly understood except in black terms. Suggesting the sharp divergence between white experience and its record and the black perspective, Cone writes,

> Regarding what is often called tradition, Black Theology perceives *moments* of authentic identification with the ethical implications of the gospel of Christ, but they are rare. When Black Theology speaks of the importance of tradition, it focuses primarily on the history of the black church in America and secondarily on white western Christianity. It believes that the authentic Christian gospel as expressed in the New Testament is found more in the pre-Civil War black church than in its white counterpart. The names of Richard Allen, Daniel Payne, and Highland Garnet are more important in analyzing the theological implications of black liberation than Luther, Calvin, and Wesley.[8]

Black history and black experience also furnish the hermeneutical principles for Black Theology. The theological norm that is brought to the Bible is decisive in determining how the Bible is read. That norm comes from a particular community, not from individuals. In the black community the presence of Jesus Christ is real and vital, intimately connected with the struggle for liberation. Jesus is conceived in black rather than white terms. *"The norm of all God-talk which seeks to be black-talk is the manifestation of Jesus as the Black Christ who provides the necessary soul for black liberation.* This is the hermeneutical principle for Black Theology which guides its interpretation of the meaning of contemporary Christianity."[9]

Similarly, black experience is the clue to revelation "[which is] not the rational discovery of God's attributes or assent to infallible biblical propositions, nor yet an aspect of [general and universalizable] human self-consciousness,"[10] but rather "God's self-disclosure to man *in a situation of liberation.*"[11] "God not only reveals to the oppressed the divine right to break the chains by whatever means necessary but also assures them that their work in their own liberation is God's own work."[12] This complete priority given to liberation is inherent in the biblical tradition, in which the Exodus is central as a political event involving the defeat of enemies.

Interpreting the nature of sin within this framework, Cone acknowledges that all persons are sinners, but he vehemently condemns the presumption involved when whites apply this to blacks. "Since whites and blacks do not share a common identity white people cannot possibly know what sin is from a black perspective."[13] Moreover, just as the event of the Exodus changed Israel's self-understanding and destiny, and just as the resurrection of Christ changed the self-understanding of the disciples, so the awareness of black liberation changes the self-understanding of black people in a special revelatory experience known to them alone.

Speech about God must be altered from the speech about God in white theology. The need for such an alteration brings such speech to the brink of "treason and heresy," and invites hostility and punishment from those who hold power. God language is not to be abandoned, even though as used in white terms it fails to point to the possibility of liberation, but it is to be kept and used in black terms to point to the ONE who sides with the oppressed in their struggle for liberation. This requires declaring flatly that God is black. Doing this makes clear that "God has made the oppressed condition his own condition."[14]

Blackness as the yearning for freedom becomes the key for understanding all theological doctrines. The yearning for freedom is not a rational decision about abstract alternatives but rather the thrust to break oppression through participation in the liberation struggle. "To be free is to participate in a community of those who are victims of oppression. Man is free when he belongs to a free community seeking to emancipate itself from oppression. . . . Freedom means taking sides in a crisis situation when a society is divided between oppressed and oppressors."[15] Sin is the condition of those who either oppress or accept oppression. Sin and whiteness go together.

Christ is black, since he appeared among the oppressed as their champion; "Any statement about Christ today that fails to consider blackness as the *decisive* factor about his person is a denial of the New Testament message."[16] This does not mean that Christ was necessarily literally black—but it does mean he was not white in any sense of that term, and that only as whiteness is repudiated and blackness affirmed will we understand Christ and his purpose in the world.

The power of this way of thinking to articulate felt injustices, to give expression to strongly embraced aspirations, and to legitimize strategies in terms of the cause for which they are embraced is very great. The literature of Black Theology is voluminous, attesting to its power to elicit response. The periodical selections alone, a goodly number of which are gathered into *Black Theology: A Documentary History, 1966–1979*, constitute a body of serious and extensive reflection. In an epilogue to this book, Cone surveys the development of thinking about the relationship of Christian theology and the black church in America and identifies key issues that are present between Black Theologians who are currently writing. He discusses the differences between himself, J. Deotis Roberts, and Major Jones over the nature of reconciliation and its role in relation to liberation; he discusses the writings of Charles Long, who argues that theology itself is a mode of domination that was not present in the black religious experience in Africa. He also discusses the position of Gayraud Wilmore (his co-editor in the volume) and of Cecil Cone (his brother) who accuse Cone of adopting the very Western theological program that has been so closely tied to oppression of blacks. In the course of this discussion he makes this observation:

> We Black theologians should not only be prepared to answer what a certain *segment* of the Black community thinks about the ultimate, but also the question, "What is the truth as applied to humanity?" I do not believe that we should limit our analysis of the truth to a certain ethnic manifestation of it in the Black community. This means that our development of a Black Theology must start with the particularity of the Black experience but cannot be limited to it. Therefore, we should create a perspective on Black Theology that invites other oppressed peoples to share with us in the search for the truth that defines us all. We must not allow Black Theology to reduce itself to an ethnic particularism.[17]

Gustavo Gutierrez, the author of *A Theology of Liberation*, reflects the hopes and aspirations of those many Christians who are struggling in Latin America to abolish injustice and bring about a better social order. Gutierrez is more politically oriented than he is ethnically oriented. He sees theological reflection as "born of the experience of shared efforts to abolish the current unjust situation and to build a different society, freer and more human."[18] But he also recognizes that theology must not be an ideology used to justify a particular political program.

Gutierrez acknowledges the contributions made to the development of liberation theology by the theologians of hope (who provided us with a sense of destiny and purpose with which to face the future) and the political theologians (who affirmed the autonomy of the political sphere and hence did for politics what Kantian philosophy did for the moral individual). Both groups of thinkers aid in the crucial task of de-privatizing theology so that the life of faith comes to be interpreted as, and lived in, social and political affairs instead of in private, interior, and existentialist ways.

To embrace liberation theology means to reconceptualize the Christendom mentality that rests on Augustinianism. Augustine's interpretation of the interplay between faith and culture constituted a true analysis of the circumstances facing Christianity when he lived, but a new set of conditions has now developed that provides a different framework for response. Among the elements in this new framework are the yearnings for freedom evident in the third world, an emptiness in traditional spirituality and in contemporary philosophical speculation, and the influence of both Marx and Freud. Marx, in particular, is responsible for helping us to sense that we have hold of the reins of our own destiny and can expect that our thought and actions can shape a new future.

> [Liberation theology] is a theology which does not stop with reflecting on the world, but rather tries to be part of the process through which the world is transformed. It is a theology

> which is open—in the protest against trampled human dignity, in the struggle against the plunder of the vast majority of people, in liberating love, and in the building of a new, just, and fraternal society—to the gift of the Kingdom of God.[19]

Gutierrez draws a sharp contrast between development (which refers to economic growth and may involve human dimensions) and liberation (which must involve a radical concern for human values). Liberation involves radical changes—changes of a concrete and political nature, which free persons from oppression.

> To conceive of history as a process of the liberation of man is to consider freedom as a historical conquest; it is to understand that the step from an abstract to a real freedom is not taken without a struggle against all the forces that oppress man, a struggle full of pitfalls, detours, and temptations to run away. The goal is not only better living conditions, a radical change of structures, a social revolution; it is much more: the continuous creation, never ending, of a new way to be a man, *a permanent cultural revolution.*[20]

The thrust toward liberation is present because man is presently developing a new form of reasoning. "The social praxis of contemporary man has begun to reach maturity."[21] "Human reason has become political reason."[22] This creates a *praxis* aimed at change. It puts groups into confrontation with other groups about issues of justice. It means overcoming the privatistic framework in which Christianity has come to be encapsulated, thus raising issues about the meaning of Christianity itself. Instead of confining herself to the task of evangelism and teaching general moral concepts, the church should become involved in political activity and teach its members that they too must give political expression to their discipleship. The "distinction of planes" that relegates spiritual witness to the church but denies it a direct political role must be overcome. "The building of a just society has worth in terms of the Kingdom of God, or in more current phraseology, to participate in the process of liberation is already, in a certain sense, a salvific work."[23] This salvific work of liberation entails the work of both priests and laity; it calls for structured changes in society, not mere palliatives. It means a willingness, if necessary, to be called "communists"; to engage in practices that evangelize and raise political consciousness at the same time; to risk the separation of the church from the established order; to accept the inevitability of conflict; and to back revolution and engage in the violence associated with it.

Liberation theology advocates a holistic salvation. "Salvation is not something otherworldly, in regard to which the present life is merely a test. Salvation—the communion of men with God and the communion of men among themselves—is something which embraces all human reality, transforms it, and leads to its fullness in Christ. . . . This fulfillment embraces every aspect of humanity: body and spirit, individual and society, person and cosmos, time and eternity."[24] Both the profane and the sacred are redeemed in Christ. Creation is caught up in the program of redemption, as is the political order that continues the work of creation. This conception of the fullness and unity of salvation is so crucial in the thinking of Gutierrez, that we quote his own statement about it at length.

> Temporal progress—or, to avoid this aseptic term, the liberation of man—and the growth of the Kingdom both are directed toward complete communion of men with God and of men among themselves. They have the same goal, but they do not follow parallel roads, not even convergent ones. The growth of the Kingdom is a process which occurs historically *in* liberation, insofar as liberation means a greater fulfillment of man. Liberation is a precondition for the new society, but this is not all it is. While liberation is implemented in liberating historical events, it also denounces their limitations and ambiguities, proclaims their fulfillment, and impels them effectively towards total communion. This is not an identification. Without liberating historical events, there would be no growth of the Kingdom. But the process of liberation will not have conquered the very roots of oppression and the exploitation of man by man without the coming of the Kingdom, which is above all a gift. Moreover, we can say that the historical, political liberating event *is* the growth of the Kingdom and *is* a salvific event; but

it is not *the* coming of the Kingdom, not *all* of salvation. It is the historical realization of the Kingdom and, therefore, it also proclaims its fullness. This is where the difference lies. It is a distinction made from a dynamic viewpoint, which has nothing to do with the one which holds for the existence of two juxtaposed "orders," closely connected or convergent, but deep down different from each other.

The very radicalness and totality of the salvific process require this relationship. Nothing escapes this process, nothing is outside the pale of the action of Christ and the gift of the Spirit. This gives human history its profound unity. Those who reduce the work of salvation are indeed those who limit it to the strictly "religious" sphere and are not aware of the universality of the process. It is those who think that the work of Christ touches the social order in which we live only indirectly or tangentially, and not in its roots and basic structure. It is those who in order to protect salvation (or to protect their interests) lift salvation from the midst of history, where men and social classes struggle to liberate themselves from the slavery and oppression to which other men and social classes have subjected them. It is those who refuse to see that the salvation of Christ is a radical liberation from all misery, all despoliation, all alienation. It is those who by trying to "save" the work of Christ will "lose" it.[25]

Gutierrez argues that the Old Testament places the worship of God in close relation to the service of the neighbor. To know Yahweh is to serve the poor. The New Testament also insists that Christ is served whenever the poor and needy are given substance. "It is not enough to say that love of God is inseparable from the love of one's neighbor. It must be added love for God is unavoidably expressed *through* love of one's neighbor."[26] Conversion to Christianity means conversion to serve the neighbor. To grasp this fact is to have a new vision, a vision that orients us toward the future rather than the past.

Addressing the relationship of Jesus to political affairs, Gutierrez warns against forcing an interpretation to fit our terms. He draws upon recent New Testament scholarship to suggest that one or more of the followers of Jesus identified with the Zealot movement, though Jesus himself kept his distance.

The message of Jesus was even more revolutionary than the message of the Zealots because "the liberation which Jesus offers is universal and integral; it transcends national boundaries, attacks the foundation of injustice and exploitation, and eliminates politico-religious confusion, without therefore being limited to a purely 'spiritual' plane."[27] Jesus did confront groups in power; he died at the hand of political authorities. The nearness of Jesus to the Zealots and the distinctive distance between them are both instructive. "The life and death of Jesus are no less evangelical because of the political connotations."[28] Because faith and political action can enter in a relationship through the effort to create a new type of person in a different kind of society, utopian thought is pertinent. To witness to the possibilities of the future requires that the Church understand and identify with poverty understood as the experience of being marginal to society.

The book by Gutierrez is one of the earliest statements of a third world form of liberation theology, but it is by no means the only such statement. Juan Luis Segundo, in a book addressing epistemological issues even more directly than does the volume by Gutierrez,[29] argues that all theology stems from prior political commitments, and even that the understanding of the Bible is affected by the social setting within which it is read. Therefore, unless theology takes into account (as much "classical" academic theology does not) the social setting in which it is formulated, it must be suspected of unconscious ideological taints, which belie its claims to universalizable and general truths. Faith depends upon a setting with political and ideological dimensions, since only ideology bridges the gap between faith and the situations in which we find ourselves. Only theologies that explicitly acknowledge their close origins in a political situation are credible. In contrast to the academic theologian, who "seems to hold the naïve belief that the word of God is applied to human realities inside some antiseptic laboratory that is totally immune to the ideological tendencies and struggles of the present day,"[30] the liberation theologian feels that all ideas are bound up with the social situation in which they arise, and "feels compelled at every step to combine the disciplines that open up the past with the disciplines that help to explain the present."[31] This means that theology and sociology must work in close collaboration, and that theology must be "more interested in being *liberative* than in *talking about liberation*."[32] Segundo challenges the way in which theology is done in the main centers of theological study in the world today.

In a volume that includes an overview of the thinking of several of his South American colleagues, Jose Miguez Bonino provides us with a more extended interpretation of the Latin American situation, including its historical background, and reiterates the contention that "The theology of liberation offers us not so much a new theme for reflection as a new way of making (doing) theology."[33] Like Segundo, he acknowledges the close connection between concrete historical circumstances and theological reflection and admits the possibility that liberation theology "ideologizes" the Gospel. But, also like Segundo, he mounts a counter-polemic against the unacknowledged ideological presuppositions in classical Western theology. Miguez Bonino is more inclined than many liberation theologians to favor non-violent action over violence, on the ground that it is more appropriate to the Christian conscience and less likely to be counterproductive, but he disassociates himself from any absolute pacifism.

A third major version of liberation theology comes from the experience of women, though it has been mostly American women who have given expression to it. This version, just as the others, involves the work of many thinkers but can be portrayed by reporting with some care upon the thought of a single representative spokesperson. We will look at the books by Letty M. Russell: *Human Liberation in a Feminist Perspective* and *The Future of Partnership*.

Russell is aware that the theme of freedom is not new to Christian theology. But she feels that the extent, intensity, and the new ways in which it has come to be felt in the present time warrant our utmost attention. That attention must be directed not only to what blacks and third world Christians are saying, but also to what feminists are advocating in the way of political, economic, and social equality of the sexes. These concerns are an extension of political theologies and theologies of hope, in which the yearning for freedom is so central. In the case of women, this yearning for freedom expresses itself in the goals that characterize the feminist agenda: "freedom from exploitation in the *labor market*, equal pay and employment practices, and quality child care for *working women*; freedom to develop more meaningful and creative styles of *family life* so that the woman is not left to live vicariously through her husband and children and is not trapped by domestic isolation from the public sphere and enforced triviality in the thirty years of her life which remain after her children are fully grown; freedom from *sexual exploitation*, and degrading use of her body for entertainment and advertising promotion."[34]

Russell indicates that the freedom for which women yearn is a freedom to be able to serve others but not to be subservient to them. It is a freedom to be able to discern critically what is going on and how to work for the gift of the spirit. "The function of *diakrisis* [critical discernment] can help women and the church to take a prophetic stance over against society as they seek to discern God's actions and to *criticize* those parts of the world (including themselves) which deny God's plan and purpose of justice, freedom, and peace for humanity."[35] To engage in such a critical discernment is not easy, especially for a group that has been expected to be sweet and cooperative, and to occupy only a listening role. It means developing astute theological understanding and learning how to ask the right questions and probe the right issues. It means having hope in a new society, in which patterns of domination and subservience are broken.

Women's liberation shares methods, perspectives, and themes with black and third world theologies of liberation. Russell acknowledges that there is a potential conflict involved in different groups taking different experiences as starting places in the search for freedom, but she clearly believes that the new kind of social reality that will emerge can cope with such conflicts. "Out of the self-liberation of oppressed groups can grow a possibility of shared world and tasks and new forms of dialogue."[36]

Movement toward such a future requires a different use of the past. No longer can tradition be a heavy weight, which chains us with a belief that things must stay much as they have been. Instead, tradition must become something that prompts the making of a more humane society—a "means for rejecting the useless past in favor of a usable past."[37] It means understanding how God sends people into mission when they sense and appreciate what God has done (and still does) in Christ—breaking with the deposit of fixed understandings and with acquiescence in oppression. Those whose story has been neglected in history as we know it will need to have their experiences told in herstory as it will come to be understood. In this way it is possible to find "a way of escaping a fated world in which the future has been closed off by the established tradition of certain men."[38] This means bringing invisible groups (those whose lives and presence have been eclipsed from consciousness) to public awareness. One important way to do this is to overcome the dominance of the male generic pronoun in our language and masculine language about God.

Addressing the meaning of salvation in terms of liberation theology, Russell follows Gutierrez in affirming its holistic nature —a nature both personal and social. She notes the meaning of *shalom*, which includes both the idea of freedom and the ideal of blessing, and indicates how the early church narrowed the Old Testament concept to mean life after death. "Liberation theologies," she suggests, "which seek to reflect on the praxis of God's liberation in the light of particular circumstances of oppression, are returning to the motifs of liberation and blessing as they are found in the Biblical tradition."[39] In overcoming the emphasis upon individual sin and death that has become prevalent in Christianity, liberation theology is making an important contribution to a richer understanding of the Christian heritage.

Liberation theologies also find the notion of raising awareness (conscientization) important, not only in an individual way, as persons are led to sense the importance of overcoming submissiveness, but in a way that critically attacks cultural realities. Without conscientization and the utopian thinking to which it is related, little serious struggle occurs against oppression. Such struggle involves attacking both the infrastructures and the superstructures that obstruct people. Conscientization involves a change of outlook that has many affinities to conversion. *Praxis,* which includes going and telling others about the need for change, has many affinities with evangelism.

According to Russell, liberation theology also furthers the search for a more adequate humanity, a humanity that partakes of the created order as intended by God because personhood is restored. The stress on humanization in liberation theologies has similarities to the ideas of re-presentation found in theories of the incarnation. In this framework, servanthood (which is an evil scandal when forced upon women) can be reconceived and re-experienced as a partnership in which patterns of authority and submission are totally transformed. This means overcoming stereotypes about patterns of work and vocation and developing a new model for human relationships. It is hard to imagine what a world would be like in which partnership, openness to others, and dialogue were the usual patterns, but this fact should not prevent us from taking the risk involved in trying to create that sort of world. It is exciting to envision and work for a new kind of world. "No one knows what it would be like 'if they gave a revolution and everybody won.'"[40]

The far reaching implications of Russell's belief that a very different future is possible are explored in her book *The Future of Partnership.* Such a future, in which partnership rather than competition is the basic social reality, would find both our relationships with God and our relationships with our neighbors transformed. It would embody the New Creation envisioned in the New Testament—a New Creation in which hierarchical differentiations based upon sex, power, or status are overcome. In *oikonomia* and *koinonia* there is an essential equality of all participants, in partnership with God. Being a partner, of course, means being free—free from those oppressions that make equality impossible. "A partnership is only strong where the partners each are whole, growing, and separate persons whose own identity is not lost, but enhanced in the relationship."[41]

All of this means reversing the Fall, which described a broken and corrupted kind of world rather than God's true intention for mankind. It is unproductive to base theology and ethics on the portrayal of human life in the Genesis account alone. "The clues to be found in Genesis to what it would mean to become what God intends us to be as God's utopia are limited."[42] Therefore it is necessary to start from the other end, from the vision of new humanity as set forth in Jesus Christ. While such a new humanity will never be entirely achieved, it is better to be guided by it than by a view that already gives up search for it. Partnership involves equality of standing, but not equality of gifts. Just as God invites us to become partners without sharing equality of gifts with him, so we must learn to form partnerships in which the factors that make for domination and inequality in present society are redirected to create mutuality of function rather than differentiation of status. "This way does not pretend that power, as the ability to actualize decisions, is absent from human relationships. Rather, it claims that in nonstereotypic or nonauthoritarian settings, the exercise of power can move from one person or group to another according to the particular activity or goal."[43]

Russell examines how the stewardship of partnership might work itself out in the realms of sexual relationships, church life, and education. Her portrayal of a new social order free of hierarchical differentiations, free even of conflict in destructive and violent forms, certainly elicits high hopes. Russell seems to have a quite different sense of the morphology of the transition than do Cone and Gutierrez. She heartily entertains the possibility of "a new revolution of consciousness in which it may be possible everyone can win."[44] Such a new reality involves breaking decisively with thinking that is dominated by power and authority, it involves having an eschatology in which the achievement of the new order is within the orbit of historical possibility and human experience. Feminist theologies do not all share this confidence. Some do, like Margaret Farley's hope that we will soon experience a transformation that will be as momentous for the quality of our social life as the views of Copernicus were for our thinking about cosmology.[45] But others are less confident that a social order in which women are more justly treated will necessarily be one in which the great enigmas of human interaction have been transformed. For these other thinkers the achievement of fair and just treatment for women is a sufficient agenda and would by itself warrant efforts to redirect society.

Liberation theologians are open to dialogue with Marxists, though they are not by themselves responsible for opening and maintaining that dialogue. Liberation theologies taken as a group seem to leave the question of violence and its necessity as unresolved as do other kinds of theologies taken as a group. John Swomley, for instance, in *Liberation Ethics*[46] has advanced an ethic that is quite as adamant in eschewing violence as some of the authors we have already mentioned would be in affirming its legitimacy as a necessary resort when confronting oppression.

John C. Bennett, who is sympathetic to liberation theology and its agendas, has observed, "I do not think that the liberation theologians have helped us much with the question as to how Christians should relate themselves to those on the other side of a controversy or conflict as human beings."[47] In some cases they have not helped because they advocate a perspective that takes one side of the controversy as the sole adjudicating perspective; in others they have not helped because they imply that controversy is something that will cease to be troublesome once a liberating agenda has been embraced. In either case liberation theology can become a framework within which understandings are developed from the perspective of the dispossessed alone —a framework that can be neither affirmed nor refuted outside of allegiance to its own particularities. This invalidates liberation theology only in the eyes of those who see a scandal of particularity as itself a refutation of legitimacy, but leaves liberation theologies much in the position of biblical faith itself—a major challenge to every order of privilege and coherence that fails by its own devices to overcome the inequalities that plague existence.

12

A Growing Interest in Comparative
Religious Ethics

The framework discussed in this chapter has developed in conjunction with an expanding academic study of religion. Many Christian ethicists have come to do their work in colleges and universities where the study of religion is approached as a humanistic field and rests on a philosophical or phenomenological rather than a confessional foundation. The concern of these ethicists has, quite naturally, focused on the relationship of religion and morality, and the functions of each in human experience as evidenced across cultural lines. There are those who would contend that such a concern is not a version of Christian ethics at all. The confessional conservatives would see it as lacking the dogmatic base necessary to Christian commitment. Others, for example some radical theologians, would contend that Christianity is not a form of religion at all, but a commitment valid apart from the usual devices manufactured by the human imagination to manipulate the holy for its own benefit.

Examination of moral phenomena in relation to religious practice has not always been a central aspect of the comparative study of religion. For example, Joachim Wach devoted a major portion of his discussion in the book *The Comparative Study of Religions*[1] to religious experience in action, but only a few pages to the specific examination of ethics. In four pages of deft generalization Wach considered the features of morality in a number of major religions—but these all too brief comments only tease the reader's curiosity. They are not even listed in the index. Similarly, in the three essays of Paul Tillich published under the title *What Is Religion?*[2] there is no extended discussion of either ethics or morality, though incidental references to both are scattered widely in the volume.

In 1965 James Gustafson, concluding an assessment of the state of scholarship in religious ethics, made this observation:

> A totally ignored area is that of comparative religious ethics. There are in a number of volumes both careful and not so careful differentiations between Protestant ethics and Catholic ethics, between Christian ethics and Jewish ethics. But careful comparative studies on particular figures are yet to be done even in these cases. Beyond that, there are in comparative religion texts some general remarks about the differences between Hindu, Islamic, Taoist, Buddhist, and Christian ethics, but nothing of major significance has been published in this regard. Again, the competence of a theologian working in ethics is quickly exceeded when this type of research and writing is engaged in, but certainly for the future more will need to be done.[3]

The study of the relation of religion to morality in the major religions of the world has generally come to be called comparative religious ethics. There may be no other way to describe it. Even though the term comparative religion has generally been supplanted by the term history of religion, an exact parallelism is not possible for ethics, since the phrase history of ethics has already been used to refer to a study of the historical development of Western ethics. The phrase comparative religion was dropped from general usage because scholars came to feel that phenomenological and historical descriptions of belief systems and cultic practices were better done by directing attention to the integrity of the individual traditions than by drawing evaluative comparisons between them. There has been less awareness on the part of ethicists of the pitfalls in the term comparative, and so it has come to be widely used to describe an interest in the ways in which religion and morality are interrelated in a variety of traditions.

One of the first books to address these issues was James F. Smurl's *Religious Ethics: A Systems Approach*. Smurl believes that experience gives rise to symbols and that the "artists of religious ethics" (as he calls them) are better at making symbols than are most ordinary people. The symbols created by such "artists . . . direct our attention to the presence of the ultimate as the really significant dimension of life."[4] Some of the experiences behind the symbols of religion are communal, some individual—but in either case they are forceful and traumatic.

The symbols subsequently give rise to thought, which creates theology. The thought engendered by the symbols in turn gives rise to plans and procedures which capture and harness the power of the symbol in action. This process may consist of steps so closely connected as to be almost simultaneous, though the re-lationships between the steps worked out in one generation often prove insecure in the next, and processes of explanation and justification occur which sometimes so transform the symbolic framework as to lose contact with the original formulations. In this case new creative artists come along, some of whom recapture the original meanings and others of whom set up symbol systems at odds with the original ones. Religious systems overly threatened by new symbol systems reduce their ethic to "an elaborate mantle of prescriptions protecting the self-serving in-terests of the institution."[5] The inherent contest between new ideas and the impulses to protect old systems creates a need to make discriminating judgments between two value orientations, and standards arise for guiding that process.

> When searching for a criterion by which to evaluate the merit of some value story, people frequently do not get much farther than taking sides with the story to which they have some emotional commitment. It may be family, church, town or nation that is the object of the tie, but whatever its object, it is always some ideal whose triumph people will promote and whose defeat they will not tolerate.[6]

Religious meanings and ethical imperatives become embodied in stories. These stories become means for legitimizing the religious understanding of reality and the morality related to it. One pattern of legitimation contends for the "rightness" of its story. It may do this by showing the continuity of the story with the sources of the tradition. In this case "the standard of truth often turns out to be simply one historical moment's official interpretation of the original set of multi-directional symbols offered by some artistic religious interpreter."[7] Or, the "right-ness" of the story may be defended by demonstrating its power to produce consistent behavior in the lives of believers or the believing community.

In contrast to those who hold they have the "right story" others contend they have a "good story." They look to the inner consistency of the symbol system and the cogency with which it portrays patterned relationships among its component parts, asking if they really work together. This approach may be better able to do justice to the meanings of a religious ethic for those who believe in and practice a particular set of standards, and thus it avoids the arbitrary judgments that plague the "right" story approach. But a still richer methodology emerges when a systems approach is taken, in which simultaneous attention is given to processes, people, and principles.

> When dealing with the composites we call religious ethics, there seem to be three main factors in all the examples I have investigated. Let us call these process, people, and principles. The *process* factor is whatever answer is given to the question "how do you view the whole process of life and action?" It embraces answers which speak of goals as well as context, finality as well as the theatre in which life's drama is played. In short, it is the interpretation given to both the dynamics and purpose of human life. The *people* factor is broadly and simply the meaning we assign to ourselves. Whatever we understand ourselves to be or intend to become constitutes the people factor. This understanding can be acquired through highly personal judgment or by means of belief in the judgment of others, or a combination of both. Taken as one of the factors in a religious ethic, it is roughly the equivalent of what some call

moral anthropology. The third and last factor, the *principles* factor, represents whatever concrete and communicable statements may be made about values to be achieved in behavior. These statements can be general or particular, autonomous, heteronomous, or theonomous, depending on the preference expressed in the particular ethics. But, whatever the prevalent emphasis of these statements, they can be taken as a set and considered as a single factor.[8]

Smurl's systems approach, which depends upon all three elements—process, people, principles—is illustrated in three subsequent chapters, each of which examines how one of these elements works out in selected aspects of Buddhism, Jewish, Christian and Muslim traditions, and in the religions of China. The chapter on *process* examines how each of these deals with time and space, constancy and variability, chance and planning, vistas and horizons, and the loss and recovery of meaning. The interpretative schemes of religions differ. For example, Buddhism interprets process in cyclical terms; Jewish, Christian, and Muslim traditions interpret process in linear ways. The cyclical perspective dominates in Taoism and in the religions that moved into China from India.

The chapter on *people* looks at the meanings attached to individual and social existence and how these meanings shape the imagery with which experience is understood and meaning constructed. The people factor in Confucianism appears in the ideal of the sober responsible scholar-citizen; in Taoism, the solitary individual who lives in primitive simplicity and in harmony with nature. The people factor in Hinduism and Buddhism is complex, and occurs in *karma, jnana,* and *bhakti* forms. In Jewish ethics since Kant the unity and wholeness of the person are made central, though the tensions between good and evil impulses are acknowledged. A great variety of views can be identified in Christian ethics since the Reformation, some of them dominated by Pauline and Augustinian concepts of the Fall, others, by beliefs in the created goodness (or the possibility of recapturing some features of the created goodness) of persons. These two views (justificationist and sanctificationist, respectively) can be compared with yet another model, that of the disciple. Smurl's discussion is particularly suggestive in showing how Bonhoeffer's use of the discipleship model acknowledges truths in both of the others. Muslim religious ethics, which explicitly disavows original sin, places great stress on felicity within and through the world.

Smurl's treatment of *principles*—i.e. of the rationale offered by religious groups in defense of certain requirements of behavior—posits that "some body of guidelines, varying from the merely suggestive to the more binding prescriptive, lies behind every institutionalized set of behaviors and can even be discovered behind the activities of idiosyncratic individuals, if only in so simple a rule as 'do your own thing!' "[9] The term principles, as Smurl proposes it, stands "for any concrete and communicable statement of a value to be achieved in behavior."[10] Using the scheme proposed by H. D. Aiken in *Reason and Conduct*, Smurl suggests that principles can exist on these levels: 1) expressive-evocation (in which spontaneity and pleasure or displeasure are crucial); 2) the moral level, in which rules or guidelines are involved, not necessarily with tested reflection; 3) the ethical, in which the validity of the guidelines is examined; and 4) the post-ethical, or human level, in which the question "Why be moral?" is asked. Religion is related to morality on the fourth level to the extent that it answers the question "Why be moral?" but religions also contribute specific maxims for the guidance of the adherents (level 2) and ways of defending the guidelines with a world-view (level 3).

A second book, published six years after Smurl's, considers many of the same problems in dealing with different schemes of religious ethics, but is more concerned to plead for a single model for understanding religious ethics.

In *Comparative Religious Ethics: A New Method* David Little and Sumner B. Twiss provide an extensive methodological prolegomenon for dealing with ethics across cultural lines. The first part of the book is concerned to define the terms religion, ethics, and law and to indicate a form for specifying normative behavior appropriate to each.

Flaying a number of classical and contemporary writers for their lack of clarity in defining religion, and threading through a series of complex efforts to do better, the authors move toward the clarification of the term religion. Looking at this task as a "conceptual investigation" they also consider the notion of "comparative" and acknowledge the criticisms hurled against it in recent years by historians of religion. They want to avoid the pitfalls of giving whole traditions simple classifications that distort their intended diversity. To avoid simple classifications they propose "*to compare kinds or types of practical reasoning in different religious settings.*"[11]

Little and Twiss then examine the nature of morality and how it can best be understood. Working toward the concept of a "moral action-guide" they suggest that "morality 'functions' to guide the conduct of persons and human groups in such a way that it constitutes an institution or a shared system of expectations for regulating behavior."[12] Morality is the institutionalized or conceptualized matrix that evaluates behavior. It involves deliberate reflection and practical guidance. It furnishes limiting conditions on action. According to Little and Twiss, a great variety of moral norms—rules and principles, duties and obligations, moral reasons and justifying considerations, even virtues and character traits—can be lumped under the phrase "moral action-guides." A moral action-guide has both a practical and an authoritative component. The practical component constrains and directs actions in particular ways, the authoritative component gives the moral action-guide its claim upon allegiance. The claim stems from both the autonomy of the moral claim and from the priority of moral matters over non-moral ones in human allegiance.

Moral action-guides must be generalizable (the authors duck the problems that would arise by saying universalizable). Generalizability means that a moral action-guide applies to every agent in similar circumstances and must apply to all such agents in an impartial way. Admitting that their contention is controversial, Little and Twiss go on to suggest that a special condition for giving moral status to an action guide is that it be "other regarding." By this they mean that morality by its very nature involves issues as to how particular actions impinge upon others with consequences for their welfare. They also examine whether moral action-guides must be accompanied by sanctions, but feel that the concepts of priority and generalizability imply sufficient claims for allegiance so that additional sanctions are not necessarily required for an action guide to be moral. ". . . a final and important point to observe about the logical features of [this] proposed reconstructive concept of morality and moral action-guide is that they neither specify nor imply any specific (normative) moral principles or code of conduct."[13] This approach helps us to understand what morality is without having to set forth any particular content for it.

The argument in *Comparative Religious Ethics: A New Method* continues by considering the concept of religion and the nature of religious action-guides in contrast to moral ones. The authors *"take a religious statement to be a statement expressing acceptance of a set of beliefs, attitudes, and practices based on a notion of sacred authority that functions to resolve the ontological problems of inter-pretability."*[14] While this might be news to an ordinary religious practitioner it does point to a central element in the nature of religion. Religious beliefs point to a certain object that has sacred authority and that engenders or commands certain attitudes or practices. The practices result from certain action guides, which are similar in many respects (autonomy, priority, legitimacy, *et al.*) to moral action-guides except they are sacred-regarding rather than other-regarding. The authors are thinking of certain actions, like "prayer and worship, and more broadly, ceremonial, ritual and meditational practices"[15] as the kind of behavior that religious action-guides point to. Moreover, the justification of these religious action-guides flows from essentially religious claims, like those of charismatic revelation, value implication, conformity to the nature of the sacred, role amalgamation with the leader, and/or mythic warranty.

Law, which depends upon a third type of action guide, seeks to keep order and peace in the social group, and therefore a legal action-guide "is a directive taken as authoritative in that it is officially both legitimate and enforceable."[16] The content of legal action-guides is directly related to the requirements of an identifiable sovereignty, but that of the moral action-guide may be judged by appeal to a broader measure of the welfare of persons and hence go beyond the requirements enunciated in a particular legal system.

The differences between morality, religion, and law are further evidenced in the practical justification that comes into use to legitimize the various action guides. In considering moral action-guides it is important to note whether or not in a given tradition they involve the inner disposition of the agent as well as the external act. Religious traditions vary in their attitudes on this issue, and the comparative religious ethicist must take note of the variation to understand a tradition. It is not within the province of the comparative religious ethicists, however, to settle which options are legitimate.

A process of validating moral action takes place in several ways. The two main ways are deontological and teleological, respectively, with sub-divisions of each. The deontological has an authoritarian sub-type in which the will of a competent leader is decisive, and a formalistic type in which the intrinsic claims of an action are determinative. The formalistic type of the deontological option may be further divided into monistic and pluralistic alternatives, depending upon whether a required duty involves one of several kinds of action. Teleological validations have three sub-groupings: 1) the intrapersonal, in which validity is tested egoistically; 2) the extrapersonal form, in which the welfare of others is taken into account along with that of the self; and 3) a transpersonal form, in which fulfillment is designated by consideration of factors beyond the self, in relation to other persons. Because they define morality as involving regard for other selves in relation to one's own self, Little and Twiss regard the third form of validation as beyond morality, however prevalent it may be in religious belief and practice. Direct deductions, interpretations, and selections can be utilized in the process of using these norms.

Vindication, in contrast to validation, refers to ways of choosing a particular action even if the choice cannot be conclusively validated by one of the models, or if such validation is not employed. For example, the appeal to the fact that all persons accept a particular kind of behavior is a vindicating argument rather than a validating one. Likewise, appeals to intuitions, to emotions, or to utilitarian consequences can be vindicating in form. Religious traditions often utilize vindicating consideration when trying to persuade their own adherents and others to follow certain action guides. The difference between persuasion (as a function of argument that appeals to the inherent claims of the norm) and motivation (as the solicitation of response by appeals to the consequences of obeying or disobeying an action guide) must be kept in mind.

There is an interplay between moral action-guides and religious action-guides. In some cases, the validation of actions is wholly moral; in others, wholly religious. In other cases, sacred impinging norms are morally justified, or conversely, morally impinging norms are validated by appeals to sacred sanctions. Our understanding of religious ethics is enhanced if we are alert to these diverse possibilities.

With this complex analysis sketched out, Little and Twiss turn to the examination of religious ethics among the Navajo Indians, in the Gospel of Matthew, and in Theravada Buddhism. It is interesting to note that whereas Smurl, who in the systems approach pleads for a holistic way of dealing with religious morality, deals with the phenomenon in the traditions gathered according to his rubrics, Little and Twiss, who call for distinctions between religious, moral, and legal elements, deal with the traditions by devoting one whole chapter to each.

Ronald Green begins his book *Religious Reason: The Rational and Moral Basis of Religious Belief* with the assertion that "religious reason comprises an extensive domain of thought but one which can be entered only by properly asking and answering a single complex question: 'Why should I be moral'?"[17] He sees this question as involving two others: 1) "Why should there be morality?" and 2) "Why should I myself be moral?" The first is rationally answered with ease; the second with difficulty.

One of Green's objectives is to overcome the separation of reason from religion, which he feels has been present in Western thinking since the early nineteenth century. The first part of the book does this theoretically, thereby becoming an updated and expanded treatise similar in its agenda to Kant's *Religion Within the Limits of Reason Alone.* The second half of the book discusses Judaism, the moral role of Christ, and the function of karma and liberation in the religions of India, with reference to the requirements of religious reason and its power to facilitate the understanding of these traditions.

Green perceives several functions of reason. The first of these (exercised by theoretical reason) pursues knowledge of the world. The second (present in prudential reason) governs choices of individuals and groups according to their own desires. The third (the province of moral reason) examines and judges choices from the perspective of the whole community of rational persons. "To these three aspects of reason [Green's] aim is to add a fourth: religious reason or reason in its religious employment. Like the others, this stands in progressive relationship to the employments which precede it. Specifically, religious reason arises because of an important conflict between prudential and moral reason, and it represents reason's effort to bring its own program to a coherent conclusion."[18]

The movement from prudential considerations to reason is a movement from the exercise of choice as determined by measures of our own happiness to choice as determined by the well-being of all. Green considers John Rawls's "original position" (that postulated condition in which a whole human family would be called upon to develop a scheme of justice without knowing in advance how such a system would affect any of those devising it). Green uses this model to suggest that we should think of moral choice as involving more than self-regarding happiness. It belongs to "the very nature of morality that it must occasionally frustrate prudence, that is, that on occasion it must subordinate the individual's pursuit of happiness and sometimes that it must do so completely."[19]

Reason can articulate the dilemma caused by the tensions between egoistically oriented interests (as acknowledged by prudence) and the claims of others (as set forth in morality) but religion is necessary to overcome it.

"How, in situations where my happiness is jeopardized by moral obedience, can I act rationally at all?" The answer, we have seen, is that I can act rationally if I obey the moral rules and at the same time hold certain specific beliefs not supported by experience. These beliefs—they can be called, for convenience, metaphysical or religious—have the effect of persuading me that the course of moral obedience may not be imprudent at all, and they render that course an acceptable alternative.[20]

The argument in *Religious Reason* crescendoes by suggesting that reason, even if it permits exceptions to rules in order to achieve more adequate service of the moral objectives sought by the rules, demands full allegiance to moral imperatives. But moral agents find themselves incapable of achieving an adequate commitment to and full achievement of the moral imperatives, and so a major problem arises that may drive the individual to "an unrelinquishable burden of moral self-condemnation."[21] Illustrating this with an example of a military officer trying at one and the same time to protect non-combatants and maximize the effectiveness of the mission, Green contends it is impossible to emerge from such situations of difficult choice with a completely untroubled conscience. Every making of a moral exception is a source of guilt, yet the making of exceptions is the very stuff of the moral life. This interesting philosophical formulation of the doctrine of original sin in the Pauline-Augustinian-Niebuhrian genre is intriguing. It is followed by an equally intriguing philosophical formulation of the idea of justification.

[The] question, "How can I ever by morally worthy?" finds its answer, we now see, in the belief that there possibly exists a perfect moral causal agency, supreme over all reality, which is not strictly required always to act or judge morally as we are, and which, in its very supremacy, stands as the final objective ground and arbiter of moral worth. By means of this belief, the individual's necessary self-condemnation is relieved and he is given the possibility—however slight it may be—of rationally doing what his moral reason commands: renewing at every new moment of time his commitment to the strict priority of morality.[22]

To conclude the first part of his book Green presents and explains a table of seven requirements of the pure religious

reason. The table does more than summarize the previous argument; it shows that reason requires that we always do what is
morally required—that the demands of religion should be consistent with those of morality, and even go beyond them. Green's
requirements locate moral demand in the will of the agent, not in
the consequences of actions, and they suggest that religion must
"resolve the problem of human moral inadequacy by affirming
that the supreme moral causal agency need not always act or
judge as we must."[23] Religious systems of morality must be
informed by a valid anthropology—one that acknowledges free
moral judgment as well as the tendencies of human beings to
assert their ends over those required by moral considerations.
Religious morality must not contradict the insights of theoretical
reason or go far beyond the knowledge grounded in experience.
Finally, "a religious system must advance and sustain all the
beliefs required by reason, whatever the tensions between them."[24]

Smurl's book advocates a systems approach that takes many
factors into account and constitutes a broad analytical examination
of many variables in the contours of a religious ethic. It deliberately tries to avoid one particular way of conceiving of a
religious ethic. Little and Twiss, in contrast, advance the moral
action-guide as a descriptive tool for describing moral imperatives
in the traditions they discuss. Green's interest is more normative,
aiming to set forth the conditions by which traditions may be
tested for adequacy according to the requirement of religious
reason. All three books are interested in the kinds of issues with
which deliberative, prescriptive, and relational motifs in Christian
ethics deal, though with reference to a broader set of phenomena.
As one looks at these three works, however, it appears that
they are canvassing issues that were of foremost importance
in Christian thinking about norms when the interest in comparative religious ethics first began to take form, and that we
have in the volumes discussed a defense of the relational,
prescriptive, and the deliberative ways of understanding morality
respectively.
   Has the study of comparative religious ethics addressed the
issues of strategy and implementation that are evidenced in

Christian ethics as the institutional, operational, and intentional motifs? Or, to phrase the query in another way, has the study of comparative religious ethics included a study of comparative social ethics in the theological sense?

Clearly, the main preoccupation of the books mentioned is in the normative direction, though Smurl does make an effort to examine socio-political uses to which the various religious systems are put. His conclusion, however, is that "it is much too easy to treat social and political questions solely in terms of power structures and tactics of change without ever attending to the stories which launched and maintain the motivating appeal of these institutions."[25] Little and Twiss have much to say about the function of law and of family and religious structures, but much less about politics and power. Green has one passage in which the justice of God in Judaism is expounded with reference to overcoming social oppression, but the main weight of his presentation is on the normative issues. Some periodical literature pays attention to the societal as well as the individual components of ethics in other religious traditions.[26] Two books have looked at specific issues in a cross cultural way, one dealing with sexual norms and practices,[27] the other with war and peace.[28]

A concern about moral agency has been a part of the study of religious ethics. It is explicitly apparent in A. A. Cua's *Dimensions of Moral Creativity,* which considers the interplay of normative principles or rules and the qualities of moral leadership. Cua argues that morality involves both the "insight of the rule model of morality in its stress on the dimension of principles and rules and the insight of the artist model in its stress on the dimension of personal ideals and standards that enter into the valuative experience of the agent in the process of commitment and performance."[29] Cua's book is limited in that he draws primarily on Confucian ethics to illustrate the power of the paradigmatic individual in shaping moral practice, but he does acknowledge the same function in other religious leaders:

> . . . e.g., Jesus, Confucius, and Siddharta Gautama, are the grand actuating agencies of moral doctrines. In Jesus, for example, the ideal of love has become a real possibility—an

ingredient possibility in the lives of some moral agents. The same is true of Confucius' *jen*, or ideal of humanheartedness, and Siddharta's *nirvana*. These paradigmatic individuals are not in themselves intrinsic actuators of moral knowledge, but they *exemplify* intrinsic actuation. We may therefore regard them as examples of intrinsic actuation. In pointing to these paradigmatic individuals in effect we focus on a concrete dimension of personal morality. We maintain a concrete perspective by seeing the manner in which academic moral knowledge is endowed with an actuating import.[30]

Cua's treatment of moral agency stresses actuation and exemplification but says very little about conscience or moral development. A book about the role that religion plays in the life of the individual by Larry D. Shinn relates more closely to thinking about moral agency in the sense it was used in Chapters VII, VIII, and IX. Shinn considers the role religion plays in developing personal consciousness. Such consciousness involves a sense of meaning which is embodied in religious myths. It involves the re-creation of experience as experienced in rituals and it also includes the metamorphosis of attitudes and intentions. The changes in attitudes brought about by religion in turn influence behavior and result in new mores and in new reflective judgments concerning the propriety of particular actions:

> . . . a founding, or core, religious experience provides not only core myths and rituals, but also core impulse(s) or imperative(s) that are externalized as the ethical norms of the religious institution. Social factors (language, customs, etc.) play a role in the process of externalization. Consequently, the end result of the process may be that the socially derived institutional ethics actually conflict with the core impulses that gave birth to them. Whatever the final result, personal and social religion interact in the area of ethical behavior.[31]

For Shinn, we must, following R. D. Laing, see behavior as "a function of experience; and both experience and behavior are always in relation to someone or something other than the self."[32] Experience cannot be directly shared except by analogy, that is, except by inferring from how another behaves that the other person is having the same experience as we are having. This being the case, behavior (i.e. moral deportment and ethical reflection upon it) becomes a means of conveying religious experience, and the acceptance of a new behavioral pattern is one test of the extent to which a convert has entered into a given experience. "The imperatives of personal religion . . . are less a system of ethics than a coherent drive toward a particular type of behavior (e.g., nonviolent or loving)."[33]

Movement, from personal experience and the behavioral patterns associated with it through reflective generalization, and from reflective generalization to social activity, results in ethical pronouncements. Moreover, the effect of religious experience (which must take into account all the activities of its surrounding culture, either by confirming, denying, or transforming them) is to involve all of life, not merely a portion of it. The process of dealing with the circumstances of the surrounding culture is affected both by the heritage of the founding impulse and by the authority-making groups within the continuing tradition. One of the problems in any religion is the difficulty of keeping these two influences in reasonable harmony.

Shinn uses the convenant impulse in Yahwism and the concept of detached compassion in Buddhism to illustrate how this theoretical framework appears in practice.

In the present comparative study of religious ethics we find a heavy concern with individual methodologies as applied by authors to a limited number of traditions. In some cases the concern with methodology appears as a thrust to find the single most adequate way of understanding religious morality and its expressions. Perhaps there is no single way, but each of the approaches has the power to unlock some understandings and to exclude others. If that is the case, the possibilities of comprehensive complementarity need to be explored for comparative religious ethics in the same way they need to be explored for understanding the full range of Christian ethics. Moreover, time will undoubtedly bring together enough scholars, competent in enough different traditions, who are conversant enough with each other's diverse methodologies to serve up a more extensive fare than is available at present. The prospects are exciting.

Academicians pride themselves (with justification) on an ability to overcome parochial myopias. The comparative study of religious ethics can enrich our grasp of how religious faith and moral practice interrelate. It can take us beyond the confines of Western ways of formulating issues. But the comparative study of religious ethics is deeply associated with the history of religions as an academic discipline, and that discipline has its own confines. It is largely dependent upon a traditional scholarly context and the study of the classical expressions of the different religions, and has not yet extensively explored such new thrusts as those produced by liberation theology in South America. Surely it would be of great interest to learn whether there are parallels in other religions and in other cultures to the changes in consciousness associated with liberation theology in developing countries or among the blacks and women in our country.

Even if a broad transcultural understanding about how religion and morality interact with each other emerges, that by itself will not settle the debates about alternatives which are the very stuff of moral reflection. It may well reveal that the persistent differences within traditions are as crucial as the differences between them. To know these things will make us better informed, perhaps even wiser about the interplay of faith and morality. But we can never become so completely informed as to be intellectually certain that we are morally right. To live by faith—by any faith or even an appreciation of all faiths—is to see through a glass darkly, and then to trust that we see enough and use what we see with sufficient fidelity to be accounted worthy despite our limitations.

Notes

Preface

1. An exemplary instance of such bibliographical reporting and interpretation, concentrating more exclusively on Roman Catholic thinking than does this survey, is Richard J. McCormick's series of Notes on Moral Theology which appeared originally in *Theological Studies* and has more recently been issued as a book entitled *Notes on Moral Theology 1965 through 1980*. Washington, D.C.: University Press of America, 1981.
2. Edward LeRoy Long, Jr., *A Survey of Christian Ethics*. New York: Oxford University Press, 1967, p. 293.

Chapter 1

1. Charles E. Curran, *Christian Morality Today: The Renewal of Moral Theology*. Notre Dame, Ind.: Fides, 1966, pp. xviii and xix.
2. James Sellers, *Theological Ethics*. New York: Macmillan; London: Collier-Macmillan, c.1966, p. 12.
3. Ibid. p. 31.
4. Ibid. p.37.
5. Ibid. p. 46.
6. Ibid. p. 73f.
7. James Sellers, *Public Ethics: American Morals and Manners*. New York, Evanston, and London: Harper and Row, c.1970, p. 205.
8. Ibid. p. 207.
9. Arthur J. Dyck, *On Human Care: An Introduction to Ethics*. Nashville: Abingdon, c.1977, p. 22.
10. Ibid. p. 59f.
11. Ibid. p. 100.
12. For the concept of the ideal moral judge, Dyck acknowleges his indebtedness to Roderick Firth.
13. Ibid. p. 144.
14. John Macquarrie, *Three Issues in Ethics*. New York, Evanston, and London: Harper and Row, c.1970, p. 92.
15. Ibid. p. 105.
16. See Edward LeRoy Long, Jr., *A Survey of Christian Ethics*. New York: Oxford University Press, 1976, p. 108f.

17. See Chapter II below.
18. J. Philip Wogaman, *A Christian Method of Moral Judgment*. Philadelphia: Westminster Press, 1976, p. 135.
19. Tom L. Beauchamp and James F. Childress, *Principles of Biomedical Ethics*. New York: Oxford University Press, 1979, p. 5.
20. Ibid. p. x.
21. James M. Gustafson, "Moral Discernment in the Christian Life," in Gene H. Outka and Paul Ramsey, eds., *Norm and Context in Christian Ethics*. New York: Charles Scribner's Sons, 1968, p. 26. (This same essay is reprinted in James M. Gustafson, *Theology and Christian Ethics*. Philadelphia: Pilgrim Press, *c.*1974, pp. 99–120.)
22. See Edward LeRoy Long, Jr., *A Survey of Christian Ethics*, p. 54f.
23. London: George Allen and Unwin, 1970.

Chapter 2

1. Harold J. Berman, *The Interaction of Law and Religion*. Nashville: Abingdon, *c.*1974, p. 78.
2. Ibid. p. 84.
3. Walter G. Muelder, *Moral Law in Christian Ethics*. Richmond, Va.: John Knox Press, 1966, p. 12.
4. Ibid. p. 10.
5. Ibid. p. 48f.
6. Ibid. p. 53.
7. Ibid. p. 72.
8. Ibid. p. 153.
9. Volume One: *General Moral Theology*, Volume Two: *Special Moral Theology*, Volume Three: *Special Moral Theology*, tr. by Edwin G. Kaiser. Westminster, Md.: Newman Press, 1966.
10. *General Moral Theology*, p. 295.
11. Ibid. p. 268.
12. *Special Moral Theology*, p. 685, fn.
13. Bernard Häring, *Free and Faithful in Christ: General Moral Theology for Clergy and Laity*. Vol. One. New York: Seabury Press, A Crossroad Book, 1978, p. 3; see also Vol. Two.
14. *Free and Faithful in Christ: The Truth Will Set You Free*. Vol. Two. New York: Seabury Press, 1979; *Free and Faithful in Christ: Light Is the World*. Vol. Three. New York: Seabury Press, 1981.
15. Charles E. Curran, *Transition and Tradition in Moral Theology*. Notre Dame, Ind.: University of Notre Dame Press, *c.*1979, p. 5. See also by the same author, *Christian Morality Today: The Renewal of Moral Theology*. Notre Dame, Ind.: Fides, *c.*1966; *Catholic Moral Theology in Dialogue*. Notre Dame, Ind.: Fides, 1972; *Themes in Fundamental Moral Theology*. Notre Dame, Ind.: University of Notre Dame Press, 1977.

16. See particularly Curran's chapter "Catholic Moral Theology Today," in *New Perspectives in Moral Theology*. Notre Dame, Ind.: Fides, 1974.

17. Ibid. p. 6.

18. Two volumes by this title have appeared. The first a Scottish Journal of Theology Occasional Paper (No. 11) in 1965, published in Edinburgh: Oliver and Boyd; the second having been revised and expanded and published in New York: Charles Scribner's Sons, 1967. All citations that follow are from the American edition.

19. Paul Ramsey, *Basic Christian Ethics*. New York: Charles Scribner's Sons, 1950, pp. 74ff.

20. From Frankena's book, *Ethics*. Englewood Cliffs, N.J.: Prentice-Hall, 1963.

21. *Deeds and Rules*, p. 3.

22. Ibid. p. 5.

23. "Love and Principle in Christian Ethics" in Alvin Plantinga, ed., *Faith and Philosophy*. Grand Rapids, Mich.: Wm. B. Eerdmans, 1964.

24. *Deeds and Rules,* p. 131.

25. Ibid. p. 137.

26. John Murray, *Principles of Conduct*. London: Tyndale, 1957, p. 154.

27. Milton L. Rudnick, *Christian Ethics for Today: An Evangelical Approach*. Grand Rapids, Mich.: Baker Book House, *c.* 1979, p. 10.

28. Ibid. p. 10.

29. Ibid. p. 46.

30. Ibid. p. 50.

31. Normal L. Geisler, *Ethics: Alternatives and Issues*. Grand Rapids, Mich.: Zondervan, 1971, p. 20.

32. Ibid. p. 114.

33. These principles are found enunciated between pages 115 and 120, ibid.

34. Millard J. Erikson, *Relativism in Contemporary Christian Ethics*. Grand Rapids, Mich.: Baker Book House, 1974, p. 134.

35. Ibid. p. 141.

36. Stuart Blanch (Archbishop of York), *The Trumpet in the Morning: Law and Freedom in the Light of the Hebraeo-Christian Tradition*. Dunton Green, Sevenoaks, Kent: Hodder and Stoughton, 1979; New York: Oxford University Press, 1979.

37. For example, Randal Earl Denney, *Tables of Stone for Modern Living*. Grand Rapids, Mich.: Baker Book House, 1970; Walter Harrelson, *The Ten Commandments and Human Rights*. Philadelphia: Fortress Press, 1980; John Shelby Spong, *The Living Commandments*. New York: The Seaburg Press, 1977; and Brita Stendahl, *Sabbatical Reflection: The Ten Commandments in a New Day*. Philadelphia: Fortress Press, 1980.

Chapter 3

1. G. W. Bromiley, "Editor's Preface," in Jacques Ellul, *The Ethics of Freedom*. Grand Rapids, Mich.: Wm. B. Eerdmans, *c.*1976, p. 5.

2. Jacques Ellul, *The Presence of the Kingdom*. Philadelphia: Westminster Press, 1951, p. 20.

3. Jacques Ellul, *To Will and To Do: An Ethical Research for Christians*. Philadelphia and Boston: Pilgrim Press, 1969.

4. Grand Rapids, Mich.: Wm. B. Eerdmans, *c.* 1976.

5. *To Will and To Do*, p. 13.

6. Ibid. p. 16.

7. Ibid., see p. 25.

8. Ibid. p. 77.

9. Ibid. p. 204.

10. Ibid. p. 245.

11. Ibid. p. 248.

12. Jacques Ellul, *The Ethics of Freedom,* p. 62.

13. Ibid. p. 62.

14. Ibid. p. 106.

15. Ibid. p. 111.

16. Ibid. p. 117.

17. Ibid. p. 151.

18. Helmut Thielicke, *Theological Ethics.* Volume One: *Foundations.* Philadelphia: Fortress Press. *c.* 1966. Volume Two: *Politics.* Philadelphia: Fortress Press, *c.*1969. Volume Three: first published under title *The Ethics of Sex,* Grand Rapids, Mich.: Baker Book House, 1975. All three volumes have been reprinted in 1979 by Wm. B. Eerdmans Publishing House, Volume Three entitled *Theological Ethics: Sex.*

19. Ibid. p. 505.

20. Ibid. p. xix.

21. Knud E. Løgstrup, *The Ethical Demand,* trans. by Theodore I. Jensen. Philadelphia: Fortress Press, 1971, p..3.

22. Ibid. p. 27f.

23. Ibid. p. 115.

24. Robert Merrihew Adams, "A Modified Divine Command Theory of Ethical Wrongness," in Gene M. Outka and John P. Reeder, Jr., eds., *Religion and Morality: A Collection of Essays.* Garden City, N.Y.: Anchor/Doubleday, 1973, p. 334.

25. Ibid. p. 335.

26. Ibid. p. 340.

27. Bruce C. Birch and Larry L. Rasmussen, *Bible and Ethics in the Christian Life.* Minneapolis, Minn.; Augsburg, 1976, p. 119f.

28. James B. Nelson, *Moral Nexus: Ethics of Christian Identity and Community.* Philadelphia: Westminster Press, *c.*1971, p. 34f.

29. Charles E. Curran, *New Perspectives in Moral Theology.* Notre Dame, Ind.: Fides, 1974, p. 15.

30. Ibid. p. 16.

31. See Harvey Cox, ed., *The Situation Ethics Debate.* Philadelphia: Wesminster Press, 1968; and *The Storm Over Ethics.* Philadelphia: United Church Press, 1967.

32. O. Sydney Barr, *The Christian New Morality: A Biblical Study of Situation Ethics*. New York: Oxford University Press, 1969, p. viii.
33. John Macquarrie, *Three Issues in Ethics*. New York: Harper and Row, 1970. See especially chapter 2.
34. Gene H. Outka and Paul Ramsey, eds., *Norm and Context in Christian Ethics*. New York: Charles Scribner's Sons, 1968.

Chapter 4

1. Helmut Thielicke, *Theological Ethics*, Volume Two: *Politics*. William H. Lazareth, trans. Philadelphia: Fortress Press, 1969, p. 21.
2. Ibid. p. 118.
3. Ibid. p. 143.
4. Ibid. p. 174.
5. Ibid. p. 215f.
6. Ibid. p. 255.
7. Max L. Stackhouse, *Ethics and the Urban Ethos: An Essay in Social Theory and Theological Reconstruction*. Boston: Beacon Press, 1972, p. 3.
8. Ibid. p. 5.
9. See Max L. Stackhouse, *Ethics of Necropolis*. Boston: Beacon Press, 1971.
10. Max L. Stackhouse, *Ethics and the Urban Ethos*, p. 11.
11. Ibid. p. 16.
12. Ibid. p. 20.
13. Ibid. p. 16.
14. Ibid. p. 52.
15. Ibid. p. 65.
16. Ibid. p. 67.
17. Ibid. p. 94.
18. Ibid. p. 96.
19. Ibid. p. 150.
20. Ibid. p. 142f.
21. Ibid. p. 137.
22. Ibid. p. 197.
23. See John R. Wilcox, *Taking Time Seriously: James Luther Adams*. Washington: University Press of America, 1978, especially chapter 5.
24. James Luther Adams, "Blessed Are the Powerful," *The Christian Century*, Vol. LXXXVI, no. 25 (June 18, 1969), p. 839.
25. James D. Hunt, "Voluntary Association as a Key to History," in D. B. Robertson, *Voluntary Associations: A Study of Groups in Free Societies: Essays in Honor of James Luther Adams*. Richmond, Va.: John Knox Press, 1966, p. 371.
26. James Luther Adams, "Mediating Structures and the Separation of Powers," in Michael Novak, ed., *Democracy and Mediating Structrures: A Theological Inquiry*. Washington, D.C.: American Enterprise Institute for Public Policy Research, 1980, p. 27.

27. Carl F. H. Henry, *Aspects of Christian Social Ethics*. Grand Rapids, Mich.: Wm. B. Eerdmans, *c*. 1964, p. 10.
28. Ibid. p. 16.
29. Ibid. p. 26.
30. Ibid. p. 60.
31. Ibid. p. 64.
32. Ibid. p. 77.
33. Ibid. p. 80f.
34. Ibid. p. 99.
35. Ibid. p. 101.
36. Carl F. H. Henry, *A Plea for Evangelical Demonstration*. Grand Rapids, Mich.: Baker Book House, 1971, p. 95.
37. Ibid. p. 103.
38. Charles Davis, *A Question of Conscience*. New York: Harper and Row, 1967.
39. For an example of post-Vatican II Roman Catholic thinking on the church see Gregory Baum and Andrew Greeley, eds., *The Church as Institution*. New York: Herder and Herder, 1974 (Concilium Series, New Series, Volume I, no. 10).
40. James M. Gustafson, "Two Requisites for the American Church: Moral Discourse and Institutional Power," in *The Church as Moral Decision-Maker*. Philadelphia: Pilgrim Press, 1970, p. 152.
41. Ibid. p. 152f.
42. Thomas C. Oden, *Beyond Revolution: A Response to the Underground Church*. Philadelphia: Westminister Press, 1970, p. 26.

Chapter 5

1. Richard J. Mouw, *Politics and the Biblical Drama*. Grand Rapids, Mich.: Wm. B. Eerdmans, 1976, p. 12.
2. Ibid. p. 67.
3. Ibid. p. 77.
4. Ibid. p. 89.
5. Ibid. p. 90.
6. Ibid. p. 92.
7. For a discussion of Yoder's views, see Chapter VI of this volume.
8. Mouw, *Politics and the Biblical Drama*, p. 104f.
9. For a discussion of the views of those who make this judgment, see Chapter VI below.
10. Mouw, *Politics and the Biblical Drama*, p. 137.
11. Paul Lehmann, *The Transfiguration of Politics*. New York: Harper and Row, 1975, p. xiii.
12. Ibid. p. xiii.
13. Ibid. p. 20.

14. Ibid. p. 39.
15. Ibid. p. 58.
16. Ibid. p. 232.
17. Ibid. p. 236.
18. See Edward LeRoy Long, Jr., *A Survey of Christian Ethics.* New York: Oxford University Press, 1967, especially pp. 227ff.
19. Paul B. Henry, "Christian Perspectives on Power Politics," in Perry C. Cotham, ed., *Christian Social Ethics: Perspectives and Problems.* Grand Rapids, Mich.: Baker Book House, 1979, p. 63.
20. Ibid. p. 67.
21. Ibid. p. 69.
22. Ibid. p. 71.
23. Johann Metz, *Theology of the World,* trans. by William Glen-Doepel. New York: Herder and Herder, 1969; Jürgen Moltmann, *Theology of Hope,* trans. by James W. Leith. New York: Harper and Row, 1979; and Dorothee Soelle, *Political Theology,* trans. by John Shelley. Philadelphia: Fortress Press, 1974.
24. Metz, *Theology of the World,* p. 110.
25. Soelle, *Political Theology,* p. 5f.
26. Ibid. p. 17f.
27. Ibid. p. 60.
28. Ibid. p. 61.
29. Ibid. p. 64.
30. *Religion and Political Society.* (Edited and translated in the Institute of Christian Thought.) New York: Harper and Row, 1974.
31. Ibid. p. 177.
32. Ibid. p. 189f.
33. Ibid. p. 203.
34. Ibid. p. 204.
35. John J. Vincent, "Doing Theology," in Rex Ambler and David Haslam, eds, *Agenda for Prophets: Towards a Political Theology for Britain.* London: Bowerdean Press, 1980, pp. 123–34.
36. Rex Ambler and David Haslam, eds., *Agenda for Prophets.*
37. See Sergio Torres and John Eagleson eds., *Theology in the Americas.* Maryknoll N.Y.: Obris Books, 1976; and Joseph Petulla, *Christian Political Theology.* New York: Orbis Books, 1972.
38. Edward Norman, *Christianity and World Order.* Oxford and New York: Oxford University Press, 1979.
39. For a critique of Norman's book see *Christian Faith and Political Hopes: A Reply to E. R. Norman* by Charles Elliott et al. London: Epworth Press, 1979.
40. Keith R. Bridston, *Church Politics.* New York and Cleveland: World Publishing, 1969, p. 101.
41. Ibid. p. 139.
42. Ibid. p. 162.

Chapter 6

1. Jacques Ellul, *The Meaning of the City,* trans. by Dennis Pardee. Grand Rapids, Mich.: Wm. B. Eerdmans, 1970, p. 26.
2. Ibid. p. 30.
3. Ibid. p. 47.
4. Ibid. p. 74.
5. Ibid. p. 87.
6. Ibid. p. 97.
7. Ibid. p. 118.
8. Ibid. p. 119.
9. Ibid. p. 147.
10. Jacques Ellul, *The Political Illusion,* trans. by Conrad Kellen. New York: Vintage Books, Random House, 1967, p. 201.
11. Ibid. p. 95.
12. Ibid. p. 222.
13. Jacques Ellul, *Violence: Reflections from a Christian Perspective,* trans. by Cecelia Gaul Kings. New York: Seabury Press, 1969, p. 41.
14. Ibid. p. 69.
15. Ibid. p. 69.
16. Ibid. p. 113.
17. William Stringfellow, *An Ethic for Christians and Other Aliens in a Strange Land.* Waco, Texas: Word Books, 1973, p. 17.
18. Ibid. p. 36.
19. Ibid. p. 35.
20. Ibid. p. 49.
21. Ibid. p. 55.
22. William Stringfellow, *Conscience and Obedience: The Politics of Romans 13 and Revelation 13 in Light of the Second Coming.* Waco, Texas: Word Books, 1977, p. 63.
23. Ibid. p. 93.
24. John H. Yoder, *The Politics of Jesus: Vicit Agnus Noster.* Grand Rapids, Mich.: Wm. B. Eerdmans, 1972, p. 97.
25. Ibid. p. 138.
26. Ibid. p. 143.
27. Ibid. p. 148.
28. Ibid. p. 153.
29. Ibid. p. 156.
30. Ibid. p. 181.
31. Bernard M. Loomer, "Two Kinds of Power," in *Criterion: A Publication of the Divinity School of the University of Chicago.* Vol. XV, no. 1. (Winter 1976), p. 28.
32. Campbell's autobiography is found in Will D. Campbell, *Brother to a Dragon Fly.* New York: Seabury Press, 1979. A statement of his position is found in

Will D. Campbell and James Y. Holloway, *Up to Our Steeples in Politics.* New York: Paulist Press, 1970.

33. Published at 1029 Vermont Avenue, NW, Washington, D.C. 20005.

34. For an overview of these matters see David O. Moberg, *The Great Reversal: Evangelism and Social Concern,* revised edition. Philadelphia and New York: A Holman Book, J. B. Lippincott, 1977, especially chapter 8.

Chapter 7

1. James M. Gustafson, "Moral Discernment in the Christian Life," in Gene H. Outka and Paul Ramsey, *Norm and Context in Christian Ethics.* New York: Charles Scribner's Sons, 1968, p. 31.

2. James M. Gustafson, *Can Ethics Be Christian?* Chicago: University of Chicago Press, 1975, p. 62.

3. James, M. Gustafson, *Christian Ethics and the Community.* Philadelphia: Pilgrim Press, 1971, p. 167.

4. Ibid. p. 173.

5. See the discussion of this volume in Chapter I above.

6. The reference is to J. O. Urmson, "Saints and Heroes," in A. I. Melden, ed., *Essays in Moral Philosophy.* Seattle: University of Washington Press, 1958, pp. 198–216.

7. Tom L. Beauchamp and James F. Childress, *Principles of Biomedical Ethics.* New York: Oxford University Press, 1979, p. 236.

8. See the discussion of this volume in Chapter II above.

9. Bernard Häring, *Free and Faithful in Christ.* New York: Seabury Press, A Crossroads Book, 1978, p. 85.

10. Ibid. p. 167.

11. Ibid. p. 88.

12. Ibid. p. 197.

13. Ibid. p. 199.

14. Robert O. Johann, *Building the Human.* New York: Herder and Herder, 1968, p. 144. (This same material also appears in *America,* Volume 116 (January 21, 1967), p. 95.)

15. Robert O. Johann, *The Meaning of Love: An Essay Toward a Metaphysics of Intersubjectivity.* Glen Rock, N.J.: Paulist Press, 1966, p. 79f.

16. *Building the Human,* p. 144.

17. Ibid. p. 145.

18. Beauchamp and Childress, *Principles of Biomedical Ethics,* p. 234.

19. Stanley Hauerwas, *Character and the Christian Life: A Study in Theological Ethics.* San Antonio: Trinity University Press, 1975, p. I-8.

20. Stanley Hauerwas, *Vision and Virtue: Essays in Christian Ethical Reflection.* Notre Dame, Ind.: Fides, 1974, p. 2.

21. Ibid. p. 35.

22. *Character and the Christian Life*, p. 11.
23. Ibid. p. 114.
24. *Vision and Virtue*, p. 44.
25. *The Journal of Religious Ethics*, Vol. I, no. 1 (Fall 1973), see pp. 5–63.
26. Daniel D. Williams, *The Spirit and the Forms of Love*. New York and Evanston: Harper and Row, 1968.
27. Romano Guardini, *The Virtues: On the Forms of Moral Life*. Chicago: Henry Regnery, 1967, p. 42.
28. William F. May, *A Catalogue of Sins: A Contemporary Examination of Christian Conscience*. New York: Holt, Rinehart and Winston, 1967, p. 18.

Chapter 8

1. Eric Mount, *Conscience and Responsibility*. Richmond, Va.: John Knox Press, 1969, p. 20f.
2. Ibid. p. 37.
3. Ibid. p. 72.
4. Ibid. p. 172f.
5. Carl Ellis Nelson, *Where Faith Begins*. Richmond, Va.: John Knox Press, 1967, p. 12.
6. Ibid. p. 151.
7. Ibid. p. 180f.
8. Carl Ellis Nelson, ed., *Conscience: Theological and Psychological Perspectives*. New York: Newman Press, 1973.
9. Carl Ellis Nelson, *Don't Let Your Conscience Be Your Guide*, New York: Paulist Press, 1978.
10. The author promises (on page 4) to write a fuller statement someday.
11. Ibid. p. 28.
12. Ibid. p. 81.
13. Ibid. p. 93.
14. Donald E. Miller, *The Wing-Footed Wanderer: Conscience and Transcendence*. Nashville: Abingdon, 1977, p. 43.
15. Ibid. p. 52.
16. Ibid. p. 59.
17. Ibid. p. 67.
18. Ibid. p. 224f.
19. Karl Menninger, *Whatever Became of Sin?* New York: Hawthorne Books, 1973, p. 14.
20. Ibid. p. 24.
21. Ibid. p. 47.
22. Ibid. p. 178.
23. Ibid. p. 187.
24. Don S. Browning, *The Moral Context of Pastoral Care*. Philadelphia: Westminster Press, 1976, p. 11.

25. Ibid. p. 21.
26. Ibid. p. 68.
27. Ibid. p. 93.
28. Ibid. p. 109.
29. Ibid. p. 125.
30. Thomas C. Oden, *Guilt Free*. Nashville: Abingdon, 1980, p. 135f.

Chapter 9

1. John R. Fry, *The Immobilized Christian: A Study of His Pre-ethical Situation.* Philadelphia: Westminster Press, 1963, p. 39.
2. Ibid. p. 114.
3. Ibid. p. 139.
4. James B. Nelson, *Moral Nexus: Ethics of Christian Identity and Community.* Philadelphia: Westminster Press, 1972, p. 12.
5. Ibid. p. 58.
6. Jim Fowler and Sam Keen, *Life Maps: Conversations on the Journey of Faith.* Foreword by Jerome Berryman. Waco, Texas: Word Books, *c.*1978.
7. There is a considerable debate about the relationship between the cognitive and affective factors in various moral development schemes. For instance, Walter E. Conn has contended that "Kohlberg's theory, often criticized as rationalistic, is more deeply rooted in affectivity than is commonly recognized; Fowler's theory, on the other hand, though explicitly claiming affectivity as a central dimension of faith, in practice actually eliminates affectivity from the analysis of faith." "Affectivity in Kohlberg and Fowler," *Religious Education*, Volume 76, no. 1 (Jan.-Feb. 1981), p. 34.
8. *Life Maps*, p. 38.
9. Ibid. p. 88.
10. Ibid. p. 64.
11. Ibid. p. 90.
12. Ibid. p. 29.
13. Donald E. Miller, *The Wing-Footed Wanderer: Conscience and Transcendence.* Nashville: Abingdon, 1977, p. 85f.
14. Ibid. p. 117.
15. Daniel C. Maguire, *The Moral Choice.* Garden City, N.Y.: Doubleday, 1978, p. 110.
16. Ibid. p. 135.
17. Ibid. p. 153.
18. Ibid. p. 371.
19. Ibid. p. 373.
20. Ibid. p. 380.
21. Ibid. p. 403.
22. Ibid. p. 455.

Chapter 10

1. James M. Gustafson, "Christian Ethics" in Paul Ramsey, ed., *Religion.* Englewood Cliffs, N.J.: Prentice-Hall, 1965, p. 353.
2. Douglas Sloan, "The Teaching of Ethics in the American Undergraduate Curriculum, 1876-1976," in Daniel Callahan and Sissela Bok, eds., *Ethics Teaching in Higher Education.* New York: Plenum Press, 1980, p. 2.
3. Ibid. p. 41.
4. Thomas A. Shannon, ed., *Bioethics: Basic Writings on the Key Ethical Questions That Surround the Major, Modern Biological Possibilities and Problems.* Ramsey, N.J.: Paulist Press, 1976, p. 1.
5. For example, *Bibliography of Society, Ethics and the Life Sciences* published by the Hastings Center (Institute of Society, Ethics and the Life Sciences). 360 Broadway, Hastings-on-Hudson, N.Y. 10706. Also, *New Titles in Bioethics,* published periodically by the Kennedy Institute of Ethics, Georgetown University, Washington, D.C. 20057.
6. Some of the works on medical problems and practice by Christian ethicists include (arranged according to date of publication): Joseph Fletcher, *Morals and Medicine: The Moral Problems of the Patient's Right To Know the Truth.* Princeton: Princeton University Press, 1954; Gerald Kelly, *Medico-Moral Problems.* Willard L. Sperry, *Ethical Basis of Medical Practice.* New York: Harper and Bros., 1956; James T. Stephens and Edward LeRoy Long, Jr., *The Christian as a Doctor.* New York: Association Press, 1960: Dale White, ed., *Dialogue in Medicine and Theology.* Nashville: Abingdon, 1967; Paul Ramsey, *The Patient as a Person.* New Haven: Yale University Press, 1970; Harmon Smith, *Ethics and the New Medicine.* Nashville: Abingdon, 1970; Bernard Häring, *Medical Ethics.* Notre Dame, Ind.: Fides, 1973; James B. Nelson, *Human Medicine: Ethical Perspectives on New Medical Issues.* Minneapolis: Augsburg, 1973; Kenneth Vaux, *Biomedical Ethics.* New York: Harper and Row, 1974; James Gustafson, *The Contributions of Theology to Medical Ethics.* Milwaukee: Marquette University Press, 1975; Robert M. Veatch, *Case Studies in Medical Ethics.* Cambridge: Harvard University Press, 1977; Paul Ramsey, *Ethics at the Edges of Life.* New Haven: Yale University Press, 1978; Charles E. Curran, *Issues in Sexual and Medical Ethics.* Notre Dame: University of Notre Dame Press, 1978; and Donald W. Shriver, Jr., ed. (and contributor), *Medicine and Religion: Strategies of Care.* Pittsburgh: University of Pittsburgh Press, 1980. See also the two books already mentioned in this survey. Arthur Dyck, *On Human Care: An Introduction to Ethics.* Nashville: Abingdon, 1977; and Tom L. Beauchamp and James F. Childress, *Principles of Bio-medical Ethics.* New York: Oxford University Press, 1979. The contributions of Richard McCormick, though not in monograph form, should be mentioned.
7. Thomas A. Shannon, *Bioethics,* p. 4.
8. The Churches' Center for Theology and Public Policy, 4400 Massachusetts Avenue N.W., Washington, D.C., has made questions about the delivery of health care a part of its study agenda.

9. For a listing of work for the five-year period at the beginning of 1970s, see Donald G. Jones, *A Bibliography of Business Ethics, 1971–75*. Charlottesville: University Press of Virginia, 1977. A volume covering 1976–80 will be published in 1981, with 3000 more citations and more items dealing with the relation of religion to these matters. Another bibliographical source is found in Charles W. Powers and David Vogel, *Ethics in the Education of Business Managers*. Hastings Center: Institute of Society, Ethics and the Life Sciences, 1980, pp. 67–81.

10. In this judgment I am confirmed by Donald G. Jones, who even more carefully documented the same conclusion in a paper delivered at the Society of Christian Ethics Annual Meeting, January 1981, and whose paper "Teaching Business Ethics: State of the Art and Normative Critique" appears in the 1981 Annual of the Society.

11. Ibid.

12. John C. Bennett, *The Radical Imperative: From Theology to Social Ethics*. Philadelphia: Westminster Press, 1975. See especially chapter 6.

13. This phrase is inspired by Weber's frequent use of the terms "cage," "bondage," and "serfdom." Also see Arthur Mitzman, *The Iron Cage: An Historical Interpretation of Max Weber*. New York: Alfred A. Knopf, 1970.

14. Benjamin M. Selekman, *A Moral Philosophy for Management*. New York: McGraw-Hill, 1959, p. 5.

15. Powers and Vogel, *Ethics in the Education of Business Managers*, pp. 7–10.

16. Harold L. Berman, *The Interaction of Law and Religion*. Nashville: Abingdon, 1974. This book is mentioned in Chapter II above.

17. See Rule 8.1 *Discussion Draft of Model Rules of Professional Conduct*, American Bar Association, Commission on Evaluation of Professional Standards, January 30, 1980.

18. Published by the Christian Legal Society, P.O. Box 2069, Oak Park, Ill. 60603.

19. One exception is the book by James A. Pike, *Beyond the Law: Religious and Ethical Meaning of the Lawyer's Vocation*. Garden City: N.Y.: Doubleday, 1963.

20. James F. Bresnahan, S.J., " 'Ethics' and the Study and Practice of Law: The Problem of Being Professional in a Fuller Sense," in *Journal of Legal Education*, Vol. 28, no. 2 (1976), p. 19.

21. Michael J. Kelly, *Legal Ethics and Legal Education*. Hastings Center: Institute of Society, Ethics and the Life Sciences, 1980, p. 53.

22. Robert J. Baum, *Ethics and Engineering Curricula*. Hastings Center: Institute of Society, Ethics and the Life Sciences, 1980, p. 1.

23. See Paul Abrecht, ed., *Faith, Science and the Future*. Philadelphia: Fortress Press, 1979; Roger L. Shinn, ed., *Faith and Science in an Unjust World*. Vol. I: *Plenary Presentations*. Philadelphia: Fortress Press, 1980; and Paul Abrecht, ed., *Faith and Science in an Unjust World*. Vol. II: *Reports and Recommendations*. Philadelphia: Fortress Press, 1980.

24. It is interesting to note that in the extensive Hastings Center series on the

Teaching of Ethics no volume is devoted to teaching about ethics in the practice of ministry or to teaching about the ethics of teaching.

25. See Paul Ramsey, *Who Speaks for the Church?: A Critique of the 1966 Geneva Conference on Church and Society.* Nashville: Abingdon, 1967; and John C. Bennett, *The Radical Imperative* especially chapter 4.

26. See Donald W. Shriver, Jr., "The Pain and Promise of Pluralism," in *The Christian Century*, Vol. XCVII, no. 11 (March 26, 1980), pp. 345–50.

27. See John C. Haughey, ed., *Personal Values in Public Policy: Essays and Conversations in Government Decision-Making.* New York: Paulist Press, 1979. Donald G. Jones, ed., *Private and Public Ethics: Tensions Between Conscience and Institutional Responsibility.* New York: Edward Mellin Press, 1978.

Chapter 11

1. Letty M. Russell, *Human Liberation in a Feminist Perspective—A Theology.* Philadelphia: Westminster Press, 1974, p. 41f.

2. James H. Cone, "Freedom, History and Hope," in Thomas McFadden, *Liberation, Revolution, and Freedom: Theological Perspectives*, New York: Seabury Press, 1975, p. 59f.

3. Robert McAffee Brown, *Theology in a New Key.* Philadelphia: Westminster Press, 1978, p. 26.

4. These six characteristics are taken from *Theology in a New Key*, pp. 60–74, but the descriptions of each are my condensations of Brown's discussion.

5. James H. Cone, *A Black Theology of Liberation.* Philadelphia: J. B. Lippincott, 1970, p. 21.

6. Ibid. p. 24.

7. Ibid. p. 33.

8. Ibid. p. 73.

9. Ibid. p. 80.

10. Ibid. p. 90.

11. Ibid. p. 91.

12. Ibid. p. 91f.

13. Ibid. p. 100.

14. Ibid. p. 121.

15. Ibid. p. 171.

16. Ibid. p. 214.

17. Gayraud S. Wilmore and James H. Cone, eds., *Black Theology: A Documentary History 1966–1979.* Maryknoll, N.Y.: Orbis Books, 1979, p. 619f.

18. Gustavo Gutierrez, *A Theology of Liberation: History, Politics and Salvation*, trans. and edited by Sister Caridad Inda and John Eagleston. Maryknoll, N.Y.: Orbis Books, 1973, p. ix.

19. Ibid. p. 15.

20. Ibid. p. 32.

21. Ibid. p. 46.

22. Ibid. p. 47.
23. Ibid. p. 72.
24. Ibid. p. 151f.
25. Ibid. p. 177f.
26. Ibid. p. 200.
27. Ibid. p. 228.
28. Ibid. p. 232.
29. Juan Luis Segundo, *Liberation of Theology*, trans. by John Drury. Maryknoll, N.Y.: Orbis Books, 1976.
30. Ibid. p. 7.
31. Ibid. p. 8.
32. Ibid. p. 9.
33. Jose Miguez Bonino, *Doing Theology in a Revolutionary Situation*. Philadelphia: Fortress Press, 1979, p. 82.
34. Letty M. Russell, *Human Liberation in a Feminist Perspective—A Theology*, p. 25f. This list is Russell's own condensation of the goals set forth in an essay by Marlene Dixon, "Why Women's Liberation?" in Elsie Adams and Mary Louise Briscoe, eds., *Up Against the Wall, Mother*. New York: The Free Press, 1971.
35. Ibid. p. 39.
36. Ibid. p. 69.
37. Ibid. p. 76.
38. Ibid. p. 85.
39. Ibid. p. 110.
40. Ibid. p. 183.
41. Letty M. Russell, *The Future of Partnership*. Philadelphia: Westminster Press, 1979, p. 39.
42. Ibid. p. 50
43. Ibid. p. 68.
44. Ibid. p. 159f.
45. Margaret Farley, "New Patterns of Relationship: Beginnings of a Moral Revolution," *Theological Studies*, Vol. XXXVI, no. 4 (Dec. 1975).
46. John M. Swomley, Jr., *Liberation Ethics*. New York: Macmillan, 1972.
47. John C. Bennett, Response to "Theological Education and Liberation Theology," in *Theological Education*, Vol. XVI, no. 1 (Autumn 1979), p. 13.

Chapter 12

1. Joachim Wach, *The Comparative Study of Religions*. Morningside Heights: Columbia University Press, 1958, p. 114.
2. Paul Tillich, *What Is Religion?* New York and Evanston: Harper and Row, 1969.
3. James M. Gustafson, "Christian Ethics," in Paul Ramsey, *Religion*. Englewood Cliffs, N.J.: Prentice-Hall, 1965, p. 345.

4. James F. Smurl, *Religious Ethics: A Systems Approach*. Englewood Cliffs, N.J.: Prentice-Hall, 1972, p. 2f.
5. Ibid. p. 12.
6. Ibid. p. 14.
7. Ibid. p. 15.
8. Ibid. p. 20.
9. Ibid. p. 89.
10. Ibid. p. 90.
11. David Little and Sumner B. Twiss *Comparative Religious Ethics: A New Method*. San Francisco: Harper and Row, 1978, p. 18f.
12. Ibid. p. 26.
13. Ibid. p. 46.
14. Ibid. p. 56.
15. Ibid. p. 65.
16. Ibid. p. 80.
17. Ronald Green, *Religious Reason: The Rational and Moral Basis of Religious Belief*. New York: Oxford University Press, 1978, p. 13.
18. Ibid. p. 4.
19. Ibid. p. 44.
20. Ibid. p. 73.
21. Ibid. p. 88.
22. Ibid. p. 106.
23. Ibid. p. 109.
24. Ibid.
25. Smurl, *Religious Ethics*, p. 126.
26. For example, Donald K. Swearer, "Bkikkhu Buddhadāsa on Ethics and Society," in *The Journal of Religious Ethics*, Vol. VII, no. 1 (Spring 1979), pp. 54–64.
27. Geoffrey Parinder, *Sex in the World's Religion*. New York: Oxford University Press, 1980.
28. John Ferguson, *War and Peace in the World's Religions*. New York: Oxford University Press, 1978.
29. A. S. Cua, *Dimensions of Moral Creativity: Paradigms, Principles, and Ideals*. University Park: Pennsylvania State University Press, 1978, p. 3.
30. Ibid. p. 30.
31. Larry D. Shinn, *Two Sacred Worlds: Experience and Structure in the World's Religions*. Nashville: Abingdon, 1977, p. 122.
32. This quotation appears on p. 122 of Shinn's book, but it is taken from R. D. Laing, *The Politics of Experience*.
33. Shinn, *Two Sacred Worlds*, p. 126.

Index